PEOPLE-FIRST CULTURE™

PEOPLE-FIRST CULTURE™

BUILD A LASTING COMPANY BY SHIFTING YOUR FOCUS FROM PROFITS TO PEOPLE

MICHEL FALCON

LIONCREST
PUBLISHING

PEOPLE-FIRST CULTURE

Build a Lasting Company By Shifting Your
Focus From Profits to People

ISBN   978-1-5445-1214-3 *Paperback*

          978-1-5445-1213-6 *Ebook*

Every word written in this book and every decision I make, both personally and professionally, is ultimately dedicated to one person. The most beautiful, kind, and loving woman in the world: my mother, Rosa Falcon.

CONTENTS

INTRODUCTION

Culture is like a baby. You have to watch it 24/7. It needs to be fed at least three times a day. And when it makes a mess, you have to clean it up and change it.

DAN GUERRERO, UCLA ATHLETIC DIRECTOR

I love that quote, and I love talking about culture. After all, I decided to write a whole book about it. Since you're here, my guess is that you also have some interest in the subject.

What you will find in the following pages is a unique approach to a timeless topic. Yes, the book is a call to action to revitalize your company through transforming your culture. However, the majority of the book is dedicated to *how* to actually accomplish that transformation—through mindset shifts you can implement today and tactical strategies that will allow you to build a brand that lasts for decades to come.

WHAT LED ME HERE

I serendipitously met Brandon Farmer six years before we would ever do business together. At the time, he owned six Tim Hortons franchises, which are similar to Dunkin' Donuts in Canada. He was in Chicago for a Tim Hortons conference, and I happened to be there to meet with someone I was dating long distance. A mutual friend asked me if I would be willing to meet up with Brandon, since he didn't know anybody else in town. I was glad to. Little did I know I would end up spending three straight days with this guy. We immediately connected on the topic of employee experience and company culture; we understood each other.

Years later, when I was getting burned out with consulting I was doing at the time, Brandon called me about a mammoth venue he was building. He said, "Now is the time. Let's work together. Bring your skillset and come consult for us for three months."

Three months turned into six months. Six months turned into a year, which ultimately turned into, "Do you want to become a partner in the company?" I moved from Vancouver to Toronto, not knowing how amazing this journey would be.

Everything I share in this book comes from my years of experience both consulting and building out Baro, a sixteen-thousand-square-foot building with four floors on one of the most competitive streets for hospitality in all of North America. In any given month, we have up to thirty thousand customers come into the building. Today, our company continues to grow rapidly. We have since opened Petty Cash, a neighborhood bar one block away from Baro. Petty Cash is estimated to do $5 million in revenue its first year and welcome thousands of guests each month. With both companies, we now have 150 employees and a projected $15 million in yearly revenue.

Our success is due to a culture known for valuing employees and for taking care of customers. This culture has been at the heart of everything we have done, and this is the culture I want to share with you in this book.

Before we knew we would one day be in business together, Brandon and I immediately connected as long-term thinkers. We have both always believed in building systems and processes that will improve the livelihoods of customers and employees without focusing on when we will be paid back. To this day, we act out of this philosophy.

Last year, for example, we handed out $2,500 travel gift certificates to our four highest-performing employees. Many entrepreneurs would say, "Screw that. I want the $10,000 to myself. That's not a good use of the money." For us, it's always about the long-term approach. You might be thinking, "What if they leave after they get it?" To that, Brandon and I would say, "Who cares? We're in this for the long term. We're building an excellent culture that will last the test of time."

THE THREE-P STRATEGY OF A PEOPLE-FIRST CULTURE

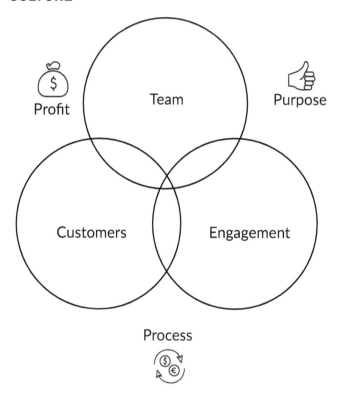

The idea of People-First Culture is quite simple—it's about people over profit. It's about building companies that employees and customers will admire. Profit is the result.

Most business leaders I meet focus too much on profits, and I understand why. Profit is important. How, though, are you going to earn those profits? Will you build the company in a way that keeps you relevant in five decades? Most leaders don't realize they aren't setting themselves up to last. They're focusing so much on profit that they can only give their leftover effort and care to their employees and customers. In so doing, they're hurting themselves.

Early in my career, I recognized that most business leaders don't know how to implement strategies for high-level employee engagement and customer experience. To remedy the problem, I developed the three-P strategy—a strategy to help you live and breathe the People-First Culture.

The strategy includes purpose, process, and profit. In short, you get to profit by starting with purpose; you identify and develop your purpose, your employees' purposes, your customers' purposes, and ultimately your business's purpose. You then build out processes to practically support employees and customers. Profit is still the end result; you're simply getting to it in a different way.

The crux of the three-P strategy is a simple truth about

relationships—prioritizing connection is crucial. We all know if we are going to ask a significant other to do something for us, we'd better be prepared to do that thing for them as well. Why is there such a disconnect between our personal relationships and our business relationships? If we know how to support our personal relationships by putting the other first, why don't we do that in business, too? In business, putting others first not only builds strong relationships, but it also literally secures our livelihood.

A POPULAR MESSAGE, BUT NO ACTION

Have you ever been to a Christmas party where you thought to yourself, *These people are only here because it would look bad if they weren't. Nobody wants to be here.* If so, you've experienced a typical outcome of a culture that lacks a people-first approach. Employees don't feel valued or connected. They are there to get a paycheck. In a People-First Culture, the central message is that your employees are the lifeblood of your company. Employees come first, and customers are not always right.

If you get that part right, not only will the company succeed, but you will be able to remove yourself from the day-to-day tasks and let your team do excellent work taking care of your customers. In turn, your customers will naturally admire the company, and the company will be highly profitable.

I sometimes ask business leaders, "If you believe in the employee-first message so much, why are you still spending exorbitant amounts of money trying to acquire new customers and then complaining that you don't have the budget to build company culture?" The reality is they *do* have the money, but they're choosing to spend it in the wrong places. A better way forward is to take some of that budget being used to "grow the business" and help grow employees.

To buy into the three-P strategy I propose in this book, you will have to take a step back and first buy into the reality that your team is what propels your business forward. Today, I'm home at 2:30 in the afternoon working on my book. My business doesn't need me to grow. I have loyal team members, like Steve Baert, Dirk Aumueller, Christina Parihar, Laura Grant, and many others. I fully trust they can run the operation. Why can I trust them? Because I have served them first.

In all of this talk about the team, you might think I don't care about customer experience. I do. In fact, I first got excited about business when I studied customer experience. Over time, though, I realized that if I don't get the employee part of the equation right, the customer part will inevitably fail. Today, I put around 75 percent of my time into building strategic initiatives to better employee engagement and workplace culture and around 25 percent of my time into figuring out the customer side of things.

In 2015, Gartner predicted that by 2018, more than 50 percent of organizations would redirect their business focus to customer experience innovations.[1] While there is no exact way to measure that prediction, I think it was overly ambitious. I don't want to be too pessimistic, but my experience with business leaders tells me that most still don't understand the importance of focusing on people.

Every leader on the planet believes their company provides a great customer experience. No company leader is going to say, "Nah, customer experience isn't for us." The message that employees should come first is even popular right now. By this point in history, these aren't new ideas. Most companies get it. They understand what they are *supposed* to do. Still, few change *what they do*.

FROM HUMBLE BEGINNINGS

I have studied customer experience, employee engagement, and company culture from all angles. I have been the employee, the manager, the consultant, and the entrepreneur.

From an early age, I wanted to know how to grow a great

---

1   https://www.gartner.com/newsroom/id/3072017

business. I thought business school would be the answer, but that didn't work for me. I needed hands-on experience, so in my early twenties, I decided to join a company called 1-800-GOT-JUNK?—a full-service junk removal company based in Vancouver, Canada that operates a franchise model. Entrepreneur Brian Scudamore started the company in 1989, and it has now grown to $250 million a year in revenue. Joining 1-800-GOT-JUNK? was my first step on a path to build companies focused on people.

In 2008, I gained clarity about my purpose when I was introduced to a *Harvard Business Review* article. The article talked about something I had never heard of before—customer experience management. For weeks after I read the article, I studied case study after case study on the topic. I was hooked. I thought, *You know what? This is going to be my thing. I'm going to build a career out of this.*

By my early twenties, I felt the itch to start a company of my own. I believed I could have the biggest customer experience management company in the world. My plan was to help companies build strategies to keep employee and customer loyalty sky-high.

When I went out on my own in 2012, I was able to work with some huge clients like Verizon Wireless and Blue Cross Blue Shield. For some reason, these billion-dollar businesses hired me, a guy in his mid-twenties. Why? Truth be told, I didn't even know how to send an invoice. I did know one thing for sure, though—something struck a chord. These companies recognized the importance of customer experience. However, most of them still hadn't made the connection between employee experience and customer experience. That was where I found a niche to add real value.

Some people assume I must have had some type of advantage to become successful so early in life. The truth is that I didn't grow up with any special advantage. Howard Schultz's book, *Pour Your Heart into It*, really hit home for me. In the prologue, he discusses how his dad hit hard times and how his upbringing motivated him to succeed. I could relate with what he shared.

My mom, dad, sister, and I lived in an eight-hundred-square-foot townhome with one bathroom. My mom worked for Air Canada for thirty years as a customer service representative. My dad had to file for bankruptcy because his restaurant failed, which caused a lot hardship for our family. At points, they would plan a family vacation only to have to cancel because we couldn't afford it. I would sometimes go to other kids' homes and see all the luxuries they enjoyed, wondering to myself, *Why don't we have that?*

When you grow up without much, you can be motivated

to take more action. I always wanted to be able to support my family financially, and today, I can. After my dad filed for bankruptcy, I was motivated to be successful. My drive wasn't about me or my name. It was about my family. If they could somehow pay for my hockey as a kid, I could figure out a way to help them. I also appreciate the drive I have because of my South American heritage. It's in my blood, so to speak, and I'm grateful for that.

I share points of my success so you can see I have first-hand experience, but the reality is that I'm a human being just like you. I don't come from a wealthy family, and what success I've had has been due to hard work. My parents could never write me checks to start a business. They could only support me with their motivation. My mom had a saying that she continues to tell me today. "*No hay mal que por bien no venga.*" This translates to, "Something good always comes out of something bad."

WHAT YOU CAN EXPECT: A THREE-PART SYSTEM

When I came on board at Baro, I knew we needed to focus on culture, employee engagement, and customer experience, but I didn't have a slogan. For the first six months, I looked for an all-encompassing phrase I could use for my team. After much back-and-forth, I finally landed on "People-First Culture." *That's what it's all about*, I thought, *building a company that our employees and customers will admire.*

This book will mirror my three-part system for understanding and implementing a People-First Culture. We will begin with purpose, which is all about getting your mindset right. In this part, you will learn to define success for yourself, your employees, and your customers. Even if you already have a great culture, I will challenge you to keep going and continuously improve.

The second part of the book is all about process. Once you have a clear understanding of purpose, you can then build out systems and processes to serve that purpose. Here, I will be sharing proven strategies I use in my own business to build and maintain a People-First Culture.

Finally, we will talk about profit—simply the outcome of the first two steps. Profit is key, and we need to talk about it—but not until we've discussed what comes first.

THE REAL RISK

You might feel that it is risky to transition to a People-First Culture or to start to take more action to align with your conviction. I believe the real risk is to ignore the importance of putting people first.

Consider companies that have recently gone bankrupt—whether Radio Shack, Toys"R"Us, or Blockbuster. Did you ever connect these companies with great employee or customer experience? Probably not.

On the other hand, when you read about companies like Warby Parker and Zappos, you realize just how much they focus on people over profit. If you don't do the same, competitors in your industry who do focus on people will quickly surpass you. Case study after case study, this truth is revealed.

In this book, you will get a behind-the-scenes look into the way I have built great companies. You will also hear success stories of many companies and people you may have never heard of before—like The Beautiful People Company, a company based in South Korea that employs eighty-nine team members with disabilities, and people like Eric Spofford, a man who battled addiction and used his experience as motivation to build a company culture that would serve others. All of the stories and examples will help you imagine how you could develop and maintain a People-First Culture in your organization.

Which company do you want to be? What legacy do you want to leave? This is a book about succeeding and enjoying yourself in the process. Ready? Let's dive in.

PART I

★ ★ ★ ★ ★

PURPOSE: FOUNDATIONAL MINDSET FOR A PEOPLE-FIRST CULTURE

CHAPTER 1

DISCOVERING YOUR PURPOSE

A high percentage of companies I have worked with give lip service to purpose and often lack a connecting point between purpose and culture.

If you truly understand and value your personal purpose, your team members' purpose, your customers' purpose, and ultimately your company's purpose, you will then have the right mindset to build an authentic People-First Culture. Such a culture will keep your company resilient during economic downturns and will allow your brand to last a hundred years and beyond. Purpose is the foundation of the entire house.

To start, consider your own personal purpose. If you don't start with a clear picture of what you want *your* legacy to be, you will never have a fighting chance at building a lasting company. We begin, then, with you, because your purpose will seep into the fabric of everything you do.

First, take a moment to consider one key question: *How would you describe your purpose?* Do you simply want to run a great company? If so, that's excellent, but I will ask you to dive deeper. *What is that one underlying value that runs through everything you do?*

PASSION VS. PURPOSE

First, let's clear up the difference between passion and purpose—words that many entrepreneurs confuse. In *The Subtle Art of Not Giving a Fuck*, Mark Manson says, "Do stuff that makes you forget to eat and poop." I love that line because he's talking about passion—what excites you, what makes the time pass without you realizing it. Your purpose, though, is different. It is a more deeply rooted, long-term value.

A couple years ago, I read an article by Ryan Holiday, and the words have stuck with me until today. He writes, "You should *follow* your passion and *understand* your purpose." In other words, your passion can and should lead you to understand where you should spend your time. Your purpose is something ingrained within you, something that provides you with clarity about why you are doing what you're doing.

Someone might say, "I have a *passion* for cycling." Great. A lot of people do. But only some people have a *purpose* for cycling. That second group of people will more likely stick with it when the going gets tough, and they will understand why they are fighting for that final mile. They will be fueled by something deeper than a simple enjoyment of the sport.

The same is true in business. We should follow our passions and do what we love. More importantly, however, we should understand our "reason for being" as we do what we love. Why are we getting up every morning to do this work? What is the legacy we want to leave? How do we want people to remember us when they hear our name?

As an entrepreneur, your personal purpose must go deeper than simply making a profit, because only then can you build a company in which you put people first. My friend, Peter "Flossy" Florentzos, reminded me of this fact when I recently spoke with him about his success as a brokerage owner and real estate agent in Brisbane, Australia. He explained he has "a passion for real estate" and enjoys the daily work. However, even more important than his passion is his "purpose to enrich the lives of families." His purpose is fulfilled when he's able to connect a family with a new home that is perfect for them, and that purpose keeps his light going each and every day.

FINDING MY PURPOSE

My purpose is for people in my life—including employees and customers—to feel safe. That's my North Star, my core value behind everything I do. It's also how I define success. I want my employees to feel like they are joining an organization that will hear them and invest in them. When they walk into the building, I want them to feel as though it's their second home.

I want customers to have confidence in us as well. I want them to feel safe when they come to any of our venues, knowing they will consistently have a wonderful experience for the money they spend. If a young couple can rarely get out, because they have a young child, for example, I want them to say, "Let's go to Baro because we know it's going to be an amazing experience. It always is."

When I started the company, I didn't have a clear sense of my leadership style. I lacked a core driver. I didn't know how to fill in the blank to "this is why I do what I do." To get there, I asked myself two simple questions: *What do you want to be remembered for? What do you want people to think and feel when they interact with you?* The answer I could give for both of those questions became my purpose. I knew this North Star would guide me each day, whether I was leading my team or building systems and processes for customers.

When people now ask me, "How do you define success?" I answer, "Success for me is knowing I have made people feel safe." I know this is my purpose, because it's not limited to my professional life. I want my mother and the rest of my family to feel safe because I'm around. I want my girlfriend to feel safe when we're walking through a rough neighborhood. I want friends to feel safe if I tell them I'll pick them up from the airport and be on time.

My purpose might sound unconventional to some people. They might not understand how it could run through everything I do, but it does. And it always will. I will always want people around me to have peace of mind and to know if they're with me or working in one of my businesses, they are taken care of. I want people to have such confidence in me that they think, *Oh, Michel's here. We're safe.* I want conference planners hiring me to keynote their event to feel that way. I even want my dog who depends on me to feel that way.

Though my purpose might sound different than you were expecting, it's an example of the kind of deep-rooted purpose that will allow you to build a business that truly serves people. When you are bringing your best self to the table, others feel supported.

Let's consider how this kind of purpose can practically lead to a People-First Culture.

HOW MY PURPOSE PLAYS OUT IN OUR PEOPLE-FIRST CULTURE

As I mentioned in the introduction, a People-First Culture should always start with your team. How, then, does your personal purpose connect to putting your team first? Here's how it looks in my business: At Baro and Petty Cash, we have something called the "Partner Promise." My cell phone number, along with the personal cell phone numbers of other team leaders in the business, are posted in what we call the "familia room"—our version of an employee break room. Any of our team members are allowed to call us if they feel they aren't being heard by their managers. This idea was driven out of my desire to make sure my team feels safe.

I recently received a call from one of our chefs. We talked through the issue, and by the end of our conversation, he said, "I feel so much better after talking to you." I love knowing team members feel they can reach out to me and that they feel better after doing so. Posting our numbers and being available is a small gesture that makes a big difference in our culture.

I love that I don't need to be on location every day, hovering over each team member. I can do *less* work because I am empowering my team to accomplish their goals whether I'm present or not. I can say, "You are supported to do great work. I will be here if you need any help, and

I'll check up on you. I've got your back." Whether it's a manager, chef, or team member who works in the dish area, everyone feels safe and empowered to execute to the best of their abilities within their respective departments, all the while using their unique skills and ideas.

My purpose also affects our People-First Culture for guests. If a guest has a complaint, and I am available to intervene, I want them to think, *He's on it. He's got this.* I want them to trust that it will be sorted out because they know I will take care of them.

Ultimately, I want my purpose of making everyone feel safe to equal an amazing customer experience on their part. I want them to see our logo on the building or video on social media and feel a sense of confidence. I want them to think, *That place is on point. They always provide a seamless customer experience. If I have to choose between Baro and another restaurant, I'm going to choose Baro because I know they'll take care of me and provide a fantastic night.*

Just as with team members, much of the way my purpose gets carried into the culture happens behind the scenes. Most customers never meet me, but I still go out of my way to make them feel comfortable. For example, I create something each week we call "customer videos." Every Tuesday at 10:00 a.m., Laura Grant, our Guest

Experience Manager, our videographer, and I meet on the second floor of Baro. We set up a camera, and Laura gives me a piece of paper. She says, "Here are five guests coming in for dinner this week. Here are their names and their reasons for dining with us." One might be Joey, who is coming with six others because his friend Shawn got engaged. Maybe Samantha is coming with friends because she recently announced that she's pregnant. Whatever the case might be, I will film a sixty-second video for each of them. For Joey, for example, I may say something like, "We can't wait to welcome you. I heard it's Shawn's birthday. Even though I won't be in the building this Friday, my team is ready to serve you."

We record these simple messages and give them to the customers before they dine with us. I choose them at random, of course, but the intent is far from random. I create these videos as a small way to help guests feel safe. Upon receiving a video, their level of confidence and excitement about dining with us increases, even if I'm not there in the building.

LIVING BY VALUES

One way to think about your purpose is to consider how to live by your values. Howard Behar, retired president of Starbucks and author of two remarkable books—*It's Not About the Coffee* and *The Magic Cup*, has always lived his values through servant leadership. I have always been interested about his journey in business and was grateful to have the opportunity to recently interview him. When I asked him about purpose, he emphasized the importance of finding what you value first. That, in turn, will help you find your purpose.

He explained values aren't just for touchy-feely people and are essential to building a business. I believed him. After all, he helped build one of the most recognizable and respected companies on the planet. Still, I had questions. *How can a person define their own values, and how does someone live within the values that they've set for themselves?* I asked.

Howard first admitted that this is not easy work. It takes time to simply learn to ask the right questions—questions like *What do I believe?* and *What do I want to live my life according to?* He's found most people come up with eight to ten core values, which in turn inform their purpose. Identifying these values, which should represent who you are whether you are at work or home, can take months or even years to do. Making the effort is key, though, because, as Howard told me, "Ultimately, identifying them will help you live a fulfilled life."

Howard even took the discussion of values a step further, reminding me that many individuals and companies take time to define their values yet don't take time to return to those values and evaluate how they are doing. We will all fall short of living according to our values 100 percent of the time. However, if we are willing to return and see how well we are aligning, we will incrementally improve at truly living out our purpose.

This process of defining your values and forming your purpose must be genuine to you. As Howard Behar reminded me, we should never come to work, put on our "career hat," and become someone else. As you move into the discovery of your purpose, I encourage you to keep honesty at the forefront of your mind. Don't force a purpose. Let it rise to the surface naturally.

DEEP DISCOVERY

To help identify your purpose, I recommend removing yourself from the day-to-day. Take away the technology—your phone, your laptop. Leave your home or office and go somewhere remote. No, you don't have to go camp in a tent pitched in the middle of nowhere, but simply get away from the daily stresses of work so you can do some deep discovery.

This discovery isn't some "kumbaya" experience. During this time away, simply ask yourself: *What do I want others in my life to feel when they hear my name?* You can then move to another more specific question: *What do I want my team members and customers to think when they interact with our brand?* Write down your thoughts. Put your notes away and come back to them later. Review and continue asking these kinds of questions. Do your answers still feel genuine? Don't rush the process. You could even hire a copywriter to help you flesh out some of the words you've written down. First, though, do the personal work. Remember, thinking *I want people to think I'm rich and successful* doesn't work. You have to drill deeper.

Through the discovery process, keep in mind that your purpose should sit above your craft. For example, my craft is creating great experiences for customers and employees, but that's not my purpose. It's not what defines me. The question, then, becomes whether or not I do my craft in such a way that I make people feel safe. Do they remember me that way? Your craft might be leading. If so, consider *how* you lead. How do people remember you?

As you move forward in your business, you can realign to your purpose through self-auditing. The self-audit is simple. Ask yourself the following: *What makes me happy? When am I the least happy?* I audit myself every three months with these same questions. These questions will help you to see how to best fulfill your purpose right now.

In my most recent season of life, I have found that one of

my happiest times of the week is Monday morning at 8:00 or 9:00 a.m., when I host "Breakfast N' Jam Sessions." I invite team members to have breakfast with me so I can get to know them better. I might meet with a dishwasher, or I might meet with an assistant general manager; the hierarchy doesn't matter. Jam sessions provide me space to get to know team members as individuals. I ask questions like, "Where were you raised? What's your mother's name? How did you get here? Where do you want to go in life?"

I'm most happy at these times because I'm fulfilling my purpose in a way I truly enjoy right now in my life. Therefore, I can identify other tasks to offload so that these times can happen each week.

Just as important as understanding when you are happiest, when you are living in congruence with your purpose, you should also know when you are least happy. Currently in my life, I'm least happy writing reports, so I always look for ways to outsource those. As a leader, you have to build a team around you who all have different skillsets and preferences. If everybody is the same and enjoys doing the same exact things, your team will struggle.

KNOWING WHERE YOU FALL AS A LEADER

As a leader, you have to know how well your purpose

aligns with building a People-First Culture. This is where honesty comes in, as not every leader will have a purpose like mine that so obviously fits.

To build this culture, relationships must be genuine and you'll need someone at the head, building and maintaining those relationships. It's okay if you are not the one in your organization to be the flag bearer for this culture. Don't force it! Know where you fall as a leader so you can know who to surround yourself with. If you need to find the right partner, find the right partner.

For example, one of my business partners, Myles, is great at what he does, but he is not the people guy. He has a finance background and is excellent with numbers. Myles would probably never tell a coworker he cares about them, because he's simply not cut from that cloth. At the end of the day, he understands the value in the People-First Culture and buys into it fully, but he's not going to run it.

In our organization, I am the one who is most vocal about people-first, and I'm the one who interacts most with the team and with customers. I'm the kind of leader who knows every person's name, from the managers to the dishwashers and prep cooks. I'll stop by and greet them individually, asking personal questions about themselves or their families. I'll say, "How's it going, Joey? How's your wife? Did she pass that exam?"

My partners, Brandon and Matty, are people-oriented as well but less vocal. They contribute to the culture in other ways—and the same is true for Myles. We all contribute in completely different ways, yet none of us is excused from working within the People-First Culture. Quite the contrary, actually; personally, I love being the flag bearer for it.

Who will be the flag bearer in your organization? Perhaps it is you, and perhaps it's not. You can only know by deeply understanding your own purpose.

RECALIBRATING FOR A PEOPLE-FIRST CULTURE

Oftentimes, entrepreneurs do not experience the joy that comes from having a People-First Culture because their purpose revolves around the monthly profit and loss statement. Central to a people-first philosophy is that profit is a result; it cannot come first.

I clearly saw this reality illustrated through my experience with entrepreneur, Farhan Lalani. When Farhan first reached out to me, he had grown a media agency from nothing. From the outside, he seemed successful, but wasn't fully content. Sure, the profit was there, but purpose and organizational behavior were absent. When I asked him about his core values, what truly drove him, he told me, "I want to grow my business by giving an amazing customer experience." I thought, *Great, I can work with that.*

I was able to show Farhan that he needed to redefine his purpose if he truly wanted to accomplish his goal. "You have to work on yourself first," I explained. "Then you can become employee- and customer-centric. The right processes will follow the right purpose."

Ultimately, Farhan was willing to do the work and recalibrate. He bought out his partners so he could pursue a new way of operating with a People-First Culture.

Because Farhan was able to do the tough work on himself and repave his path, his company, Market One Media Group, is highly successful today. He's grown it to tens of millions of dollars in revenue. His employees love him. They love coming into work each day, as does he. His customers love him too. They are loyal and have a truly amazing experience working with him.

As you set the foundation for a People-First Culture, you may need to make similar uncomfortable shifts in your mindset and leadership team. For example, when Brandon asked me to become a partner at Baro, I was on board. However, I did not agree about bringing everyone from his existing management team from a different restaurant to Baro. When I met them, I told him certain individuals were not going to fit because they simply weren't people-centric.

I said, "Brandon, if you're going to build the type of company you said you want to build, you can't have these people here. They go against everything we believe in." Today, only two people from that entire original management team are still at Baro.

Many business leaders understand these struggles. They think, "I have Kimberly in that position. I'm paralyzed by the thought of losing her because she's been here for five years." The problem, though, is that if Kimberly doesn't fit with a People-First Culture, she won't be able to perform optimally within one.

In a transition to a People-First Culture, you may have to make difficult adjustments. Not everyone has to be the flag bearer for the culture, but everyone does need to fully buy into it. Remember, first, you have to be ready to recalibrate so profit is no longer your purpose. Second, you have to be willing to let go of those who aren't able to do the same.

WILL SMITH'S WORDS ON PURPOSE

Finding your purpose isn't just for business people like

you and me. Will Smith, the West Philadelphian born and raised turned Bel-Air mega star, posted a video on Instagram discussing how a person can find their purpose.

In the video, he explained how a big part of finding our mission, purpose, and meaning comes from exploring and experiencing. He believes the universe teaches through experience and that we must explore and experience to open the dialogue with the universe and get our answers. He also talked about creating and relating. We have the opportunity to create something, use our gifts, and give them to the world. We can create best by understanding the relationship among ourselves, the rest of the universe, and our human family.

Here's how I decipher Will's message: ask yourself how your contribution to the people around you can make them wiser and more successful. When I did my own deep discovery and asked myself this question, along with the others listed in this chapter, I arrived at the following personal mission and values—which proved to be directly aligned to my purpose.

MY MISSION

To serve others without the thought of reciprocation while inspiring others to do the same. Confidently knowing that the universe will serve us too.

Learn: Every outcome, good or bad, is a learning experience. Move forward and apply this newfound knowledge. Never look back with regret or celebrate success for too long.

Invest: In your mind, body, and soul.

Persistence: Go for it. Really go for it if it's something you want for yourself and others.

Long-term: No short-term thinking. Every decision you make is predicated on long-term value for yourself and those around you.

Honesty: Have the highest of integrity and always be honest. Even if it makes you or others uncomfortable.

What is your mission? What are your values? What is your purpose? Once you find your purpose, you are then able to help employees find theirs. We will explore ways to empower your employees in the next chapter to further develop the structure for a lasting People-First Culture.

========= **CHAPTER 2** =========

HELPING EMPLOYEES FIND THEIR PURPOSE

I believe language matters when it comes to building a People-First Culture. In my business, I'm a language crusader and expect my team to be as well. I especially care about language when talking about employees, who we actually call team members. I only use "employee" in the title of the chapter because that term is most recognizable.

Here are a few other examples of how we change language in our business:

- Team, not Staff
- Heart of House, not Back of House
- Face of House, not Front of House
- Dish Area, not Dish Pit
- Guest, not Client or Customer (relevant in the restaurant industry)

- Education and Development, not Training (will discuss why later in the book)

Why do we never use the word "staff" to refer to employees? The word "staff" originated in the 1800s to refer to a "group of assistants." My team members aren't assistants to me. In my opinion, they are more integral to the company than I am. While our most consistent guests may not know my name, they would recognize if Yasmin, Zach, or any other team members who are regularly on site were to leave.

If you're going to have a People-First Culture, you must value your team above all else. We began the book by talking about your purpose for a reason. You can't effectively lead your team members to *their* purpose unless you first know how to find your own purpose. That said, now is when we truly begin to move toward the outward focus required to build a People-First Culture.

A NOTE ON BEING A BENEVOLENT LEADER

In order to lead your team members to their purpose, you must first understand what it means to be a benevolent leader. The dictionary definition of benevolence is the quality of being well-meaning. A benevolent leader puts their team members' individual definitions of success and purpose before their own. I have my purpose as a leader, but it comes secondary to the purposes of those who report to me. If I can get my team members to achieve their purposes, then I achieve my purpose as well. If I help them achieve their goals, I can achieve my goals, such as building a reputation as an admired brand.

I see Richard Branson as a benevolent leader. He has built many successful companies, and I've never heard about him belittling employees or berating them. He leads by example and is a well-meaning person. The opposite would be a hothead like Gordon Ramsey, who uses aggression to try to get the most out of his employees.

To be an effective leader in a People-First Culture, you need the same connection-driven mentality you use in your personal relationships. This is why I don't believe our team members work *for* us. I never say that. Instead, I say they work *with* us. I would even go so far to say we work *for* our team. When I hear leaders say, "My employees work for me," I think, *What about your relationship with your spouse, or your best friend, or your uncle? Do they work for you, or is the relationship mutually beneficial? Aren't mutually beneficial relationships the most effective and strongest relationships?* I don't believe there should be a separation between business and personal relationships. At the end of the day, it's all about human behavior. What behavior do you choose?

As Howard Behar reflected on Starbucks, he said, "Taking

care of your people isn't about money; it's about who you are and how you act. There are people that care about people and others that only care about themselves. It's who you are."

LEADING THEM TO THEIR PURPOSE

Often, employees don't know what their purpose is. They might have some vague thoughts about what they want to do in their career, but you can help them discover their deeper motivations, just as you did. As a benevolent leader, you want them to know their purpose.

I am glad to guide team members through the same questions I asked of myself to find my own purpose. I encourage you to find space to do this with your team members, too. While you should invest time into helping employees find their deeper purposes, as you have, I encourage you to focus on how to best help them in their goals connected to that purpose. That is often where you can most practically serve them.

At most restaurants, if an employee told the leader they had a deep desire to one day start their own restaurant, the leader would have a negative reaction. From a leadership perspective, I understand the argument that team members need to get behind the company mission, and I agree everyone should work together toward common goals. At the same time, I believe in supporting my team members individually.

When my business partners and I discuss culture, we say, "Our team members come before the company's success." And we mean it. We know our success is going to be an outcome of their success. Yes, there will be some team members who will want to start their own business someday, and they will. They might even do it with some of our investment! I have had conversations with team members in which I say, "You want to start your own restaurant? Awesome! Feel free to use our frameworks. Just give us the opportunity to invest. That's all we ask."

I actively choose to not occupy my mind with paranoia or "what ifs." *What if I get burned one day? What if someone is downloading all of our recipes to Dropbox? What if?* I'm not so naive to believe I can't get burned, but I choose to believe the best of people. First, I know we hire great people, but I also want to believe the best of my team.

EDUCATING AND INVESTING IN PEOPLE EVEN IF THEY LEAVE

I believe so strongly in the idea of supporting employees in their purpose that I believe in the idea of educating and investing in them even if they leave. Jordan, our marketing manager, is an excellent example of this concept in action.

Jordan went through a lengthy interview process. We started with fifty candidates, and when it came down to him, I asked him to tell me his purpose. I asked him what his goals were for five years down the road.

"In three to five years, I want to have started my own digital marketing agency," he said.

To me, his answer told me one thing. If I haven't gotten Jordan to his goal in three to five years—and I still have time as of writing this book—then I have failed. Helping him get to that goal is one of my personal key performance indicators. I've already started giving Jordan clients on the side so he can get ready. Even though I know I will have to replace him, I am going to help him achieve his goal.

I believe that the short-term pain of having to replace someone like Jordan will lead to long-term success for our organization. Not only has Jordan been promoted within our company—from marketing coordinator to marketing manager—thereby offering us more value while he is here, but others in the company see we have their best interest in mind. We build our reputation as a place that truly values people by actually valuing people—people like Jordan.

In addition, my business partners and I actively seek out ways to share our knowledge with our team. As we do, our teams offer more value to our company, and the company functions as a springboard to success for team members, whether they remain or leave. In this model, we educate people well enough so they can leave, but also treat them so well that they won't want to leave. Of course, we love when people want to stay, but we only want them to stay as long as staying aligns with their purpose. While they are here, we want them to love what they're doing. Otherwise, no one is winning.

This model comes from Richard Branson. His basic message is this: *If you want to come be part of our culture, you will feed off of our success, whether you stay or go. Either way, you will look at our organization as an entity that aided your success. If you prefer to grow within the organization and become a senior executive one day, then stay here. If you move on to something new, you will still get the same level of attention, education, and nurturing.*

Having this kind of philosophy toward your team members will ultimately reflect well on your brand. Your people will always remember you. It's the same as attending a great college and having a great experience. Even when you're fifty or sixty years old, you're still dreaming about your college days.

BACK TO RELATIONSHIPS

A lot of what I'm sharing here comes back to the basics of relationships.

If you knew your best friend was going to die, would you stop investing in your relationship with her? Of course not. In fact, all your friends and family members are eventually going to die. You know that, but you don't retract from those relationships—you keep nurturing them.

In the same way, even if we know a team member of ours is going to leave the organization, we don't immediately take away their resources and stop paying attention to them. We don't think, *That person is leaving, so screw them.* I don't understand why so many business leaders approach their team members as if they aren't human.

At Baro, we spend six figures a year educating our team members for them to leave one day. I want each person to think, *This company is paying me, and I'm learning. I'm getting the better end of the deal.* We even host a learning development session about finding a mentor through networking, so team members can learn how to network better. Might a team member meet someone through networking who takes them away from us? It's possible, and I'm okay with that. I would support the decision and make sure we stay connected.

Trying to limit and control people is not what a benevolent leader does. It's not how you build a People-First Culture. We have known people would leave our organization, and we kept serving them right up to the day they left. I still meet with some of those individuals for breakfast. I care about them as people just like I always have, even if they don't want to work with me anymore; it's simply my DNA as a leader. It doesn't change overnight because someone chooses to go a different direction in their career. If they do, good for them!

SUPPORTED TO SUCCEED AT 1-800-GOT-JUNK?

As I mentioned in the introduction, I started my own journey in business at 1-800-GOT-JUNK? in my early twenties. At first, I was making ten dollars an hour. I was willing to take such low pay because I knew that 1-800-GOT-JUNK?, at the time, was a quarter-billion-dollar company, franchised, with thousands of employees, and was only going to keep growing. Sure enough, they have, now a $250 million company.

I thought, *Why don't I go work for a company that grew from humble beginnings to something great?* I knew I could start on the ground floor and work my way up. I was glad to get paid, contribute, and learn at the same time. I was drawn to the company because it was a pioneer for focusing on company culture. The leaders of the company were talking about culture long before I got there, and I had a front-row seat to see how the culture was created and the economic outcomes of that effort.

After working in the call center, I transitioned departments, eventually reporting to the vice president of operations. To this day, I'm grateful for people who saw my potential and wanted me to progress. In particular, one man named Patrick Louis helped pave my path. When I told him customer experience management was going to be my thing, he expedited my growth. I mention him here because I believe it is important to recognize, whenever we have the opportunity, just how important relationships are in our lives.

Working in operations, I got a behind-the-scenes look at the making of customer experience strategies and processes. I spent a couple years in that department and learned so much. For example, I understood why our Net Promoter Score—an industry standard to measure employee satisfaction—was eighty-four, which is extremely high for any company. I also got to be part of building a Complaint Resolution System that reduced customer complaints by 33 percent in one quarter.

Eventually, when I wanted to launch out on my own, I was ready. I handed in my notice and went for it. Soon enough, I had my first client—Ferguson Moving and Storage. At the time, they were a $7 million local moving company in Vancouver, and they hired me to build employee onboarding and customer-centric learning material. I essentially created handbooks for their employees. It was my first gig; the pay was fair, and I was in business.

I continued working for various companies in Vancouver, like Farhan Lalani's Market One Media. At the same time, I was blogging on my website and LinkedIn. One day, I thought my friends were pulling a prank on me when, on the other end of the phone, someone from Verizon was telling me they wanted me to work with their retail managers in their western division. Of course, I jumped on board. I created and delivered education material for hundreds of retail managers. From that point forward, my clients got bigger and bigger.

During my early days at 1-800-GOT-JUNK?, I was being actively recruited by other companies. I could have made more money at another organization in Vancouver, but rather than take the extra $2 to $3 an hour, I stayed. I was getting a full education to be an entrepreneur.

I had a long-term view of success. As I worked, I also read case studies and learned from other successful entrepreneurs. I knew the work I put in early in life would determine what the rest of my life would look like, and I was willing to make a few sacrifices to invest in my future.

Even when I was working in the call center making a modest wage, I found ways to invest in my future. At one point, I paid for a flight to and from Zappos, one of the companies I was studying at the time, because I wanted to learn more about how the leaders developed their company culture and amazing customer experience. I had very little money, but I knew such an education would be important. It was.

I knew I was going to take that education and apply it someday to make more money than those other companies were offering me, so I stayed at 1-800-GOT-JUNK? for six years. I had a clear understanding of my purpose—to use the company as my university to learn entrepreneurship—and the company supported me in my purpose. To this day, I still acknowledge them because of how they invested into my future—a hallmark of a People-First Culture.

PURPOSE OVER PAY: HELPING EMPLOYEES SEE LONG TERM

Not all employees will see the long-term game. Of course, pay is always part of the equation. Money matters. We live in the third-largest city in North America, and it's expensive. We know people have to make a living, and we want them to be able to do that. Still, I look for people who don't want to solely chase money. If someone doesn't have an individual purpose that goes beyond money, they won't be able to share our company's purpose either. Like business leaders who focus only on profit, these individuals can't see past the pay.

The truth is that team members who do stay are able to earn much more, long term. Still, no company gets a 100 percent adoption rate on the idea of purpose over pay. In this process of building a different kind of company, you'll lose some people who can't buy into a bigger purpose. However, you'll gain a team that is committed to purpose, and you'll be able to feel the difference in everything you do.

CHAPTER 3

UNDERSTANDING CUSTOMER PURPOSE

Just as every team member has a different purpose, so does each customer. No two customers are alike. If you treat them like they are, you will never have a People-First Culture.

When my mother engages a company as a customer, she wants to be friends with everyone there. When she goes to the bank, she's going to talk to the bank teller about how pretty her blouse is. She'll ask where the teller got the blouse, and a fifteen-minute conversation begins. When she goes to the grocery store, she's going to talk to the clerk about the local sports scene—another fifteen minutes, and well-spent.

Her purpose is to have engaging conversations with the

people she interacts with in her life, and she carries that into her purpose as a customer too. She would be highly turned off by a company that didn't engage her in these kinds of off-topic conversations. I, on the other hand, am the exact opposite. Making small-talk connections with strangers doesn't build customer loyalty for me. When I'm doing business with a company, I want my interactions to be transactional. I don't need to talk about the weather. I know it's sunny outside; I don't need the bank teller to point that out. I'm not trying to be rude, but my purpose as a customer is to save as much time as possible during a transaction, so I can spend more time with friends, exercising, petting my dog, or doing something else that I actually want to be doing.

When you learn to recognize the individual purposes of your customers, you will be able to serve them the way they want to be served. Too many companies abide by "rules" for treating customers—rules that don't work. For example, some companies tell their employees to treat each customer the way they would treat their grandmother. While that might work in a handful of businesses for a handful of customers, it's mostly a ridiculous idea. My grandmother wanted me to have tea with her for three hours; I don't want to assume my customers want to do the same.

THREE CUSTOMER PERSONALITY TYPES

To help in understanding different high-level purposes of customers—essentially how customers want to engage—I group them into three main customer personalities—the director, the socializer, and the passive customer.

I came up with these personality types when I worked in the call center at 1-800-GOT-JUNK?. Some days, I would take almost a hundred calls. I would talk to people from Alberta, New York, Miami, and Sydney. Each person had a different background and a completely different perspective on life. Through that experience, I began to develop my philosophy about customer experience, noting how different customers have different motivations and different definitions of success.

I couldn't use the same dialogue with every customer, so I started documenting these personality types to direct the style of the conversation. If I was talking with someone like my friend Aleem Ahamed, I would know the person had a director-style personality. This type of customer is akin to a military general—he or she wants to get straight to the point. The socializer, on the other hand, is more like my mom. If I was talking to someone like Ellen DeGeneres, I would know she was a socializer. Someone with the passive customer personality is harder to interact with. If you ask them, "How's your day going?" they will respond, "Good," but they won't ask you about your day. They are guarded and timid. Some people become this way only when interacting as a customer in certain situations. When I used to go buy a car, for example, I would become a passive person. I didn't trust anybody because of past experiences.

When you know the customer's purpose, when you get the individualized piece right, you earn customer loyalty. Your customers are going to gain confidence in your brand. They will think, *This company gets me. They know how I like to be served.*

In the restaurant industry, there are always young couples with children who only get to go out once a month. They have many choices here in our large North American city about where they will dine and be entertained. If they're going to spend their time and money with us, we're going to make sure the evening will go well. Given that their time is scarce, we want them to feel confident about the experience they will have with us, so they'll be willing to make that purchase. When they feel we understand who they are and their purpose, their choice is much easier to make.

THE TEN-SECOND RULE

As a leader, it is your responsibility to help your team members better understand these different customer personalities from the first day on the job, whether they are in sales, marketing, customer service, or any other department. They will interact with a customer at some point, whether once a day or a hundred times a day, so they must understand how to respond to different personality types.

In our business, we teach team members to pinpoint a customer's personality type within ten seconds of saying hello—a small act that helps them better engage with the customer. In our restaurants, our guest experience manager will document the customer personality whenever she reads an email or answers the phone. She puts the information in a customer file so our team can be better prepared. When the server or bartender greets that individual, they know beforehand how to best serve them. They might think, *Okay, table twenty-one has a director-style personality type, so I need to remember they want to get straight to the point.*

In addition, we always relay personality type information from department to department to make sure our team is positioned for success. This system isn't 100 percent foolproof, but it does help.

While we educate each team member to interact effectively with each customer personality type, we do have some experts on our team who are especially good with certain personalities. For example, if we know Zach is amazing at dealing with a socializer personality, she becomes our in-house expert for these types of customers. If we know Christina is amazing at dealing with director-type personalities, we might provide some space for teaching and let her talk about how to serve those types. That said, we don't say, "Christina is the expert at director personalities, so step aside, Jimmy, and she will take it from here." Jimmy will never learn if we do that.

All team members must be prepared to interact with each personality type because our natural inclination for how we want to interact with customers is often determined by mood. If I'm in a happy-go-lucky mood, I might be happy to deal with a socializer personality and think, *Yes, I'll talk to you for fifteen minutes about random topics.* On other days, I might think, *Not today. Give me a director type. Let's get down to it.*

While it would be funny to place the same personality types in one section of the restaurant and deal with them differently, it would throw off the balance of the workplace; this is true for any business. The purpose of knowing the types is not to formulaically segment them. Each person should still be addressed uniquely. They're more than a "type." The purpose of such identification is simply to know how to better respond to them as you interact.

MANAGING INTERACTIONS

Preparing employees to deal with all kinds of customers, whatever personality category they are in, is both simple and difficult. The simple part, which we can all agree on, is that you have to deliver personalized services to each customer so they don't feel like they're getting a blanket experience. To do this, you have to understand each customer's purpose and definition of success.

We make sure we give our team members direct education in this area. I find it absurd when business leaders say education for employees is too expensive. Your team members will speak to more customers in a day than a typical leader will in a month, quarter, or even a year. Companies find the budget to send executive teams to retreats for tens of thousands or even hundreds of thousands of dollars, but they can't find the budget to educate one of their greatest assets—their employees. Here, we do just the opposite. We always find the budget to educate our first most-valuable asset—our employees—for our second most-valuable asset—our customers.

Setting up your team members so they can deliver great experiences will help them succeed. They will earn more and customers will feel better. If you're in sales and you're able to deliver a great personal experience to your customer, you earn customer loyalty. That customer is more likely to come back to you. The same rule applies across the board for people in every department.

PURPOSE-SEEKING CUSTOMERS

Some customers want to do business with "for a cause" companies; that is their purpose as a customer. These types of customers probably know about TOMS Shoes, for example, which gives away a pair of shoes for every pair they sell. They will choose TOMS because they want to support the cause.

As we are all becoming more aware of ways our companies can help or hurt people and the environment, we must be prepared to respond. The way you respond can be simple. For example, we were one of the first restaurants in Toronto to get rid of drinking straws, and we received positive social media commentary for taking the lead. Now, everyone is doing it. With this simple choice, we eliminated waste, which we did out of a genuine response to data that showed the shocking amount of waste created by plastic straws in landfills and in the ocean.

While our company doesn't focus on philanthropy, this initiative didn't require much heavy lifting and was great for the environment. As a purpose-focused company, we decided to do the right thing.

FOCUSING ON RISING GENERATIONS

A recent study by Deloitte included the following findings:

> Having come of age in an uncertain economy and growing alarm for the climate, Millennials are the ones driving demand for more purpose-driven brands (with Generation Z following quickly behind). Younger adults are the most willing respondents to pay extra for sustainable goods—almost three-out-of-four Millennials in Nielsen's latest findings. As employees, Millennials are also rewarding higher-purpose businesses with their notoriously fickle loyalty. Millennials are an increasingly large component of the workforce, on their way to 75% of the global workforce by 2025. But given the chance, 66% of Millennials around the world expect to leave their workplace in the next 5 years. Their high ideals can be key to keeping them around: 87% believe the success of a business should be measured in terms of more than just its financial performance. Of company attributes given by Millennials who do plan to stick around, one of the most frequently cited is "a strong sense of purpose beyond financial success."

Some companies are more actively prepared to serve an increasing population of purpose-seeking customers today. Pela Case is a biodegradable cell phone case, for example, and the company is growing like crazy. They serve a huge community of environmentally conscious consumers, many of whom will only buy products from companies that serve the planet.

When I interviewed Matt Bertulli, who runs Pela Case, he said, "As an outdoor enthusiast, I always had this thought there are better ways to do business. I saw an interesting opportunity to take a big category and reinvent it completely. It was all about the environmental impact. The audience came naturally."[2]

"Zero Wasters" is a new term for those who try to not produce any waste in their day-to-day lives. What that usually means is they don't buy anything that's throwaway, and if they do buy something that's throw-away, it needs to go away gracefully by being compostable or biodegradable. These people, many of whom are in younger generations, don't use any plastic. If they buy a bottle, it's a water bottle that'll last twenty-five years. They're trying to have the least amount of impact on their planet.

Whether you are considering how a customer prefers to interact or how they hope to save the planet, purpose matters when it comes to customers, just as much as it matters for you and your employees. As you consider all three purposes, you will ultimately be better equipped to understand your company's purpose.

CHAPTER 4

WHAT'S YOUR COMPANY'S PURPOSE?

What do you want your company to represent? What do you want your legacy to be? Commit to the vision, and the economics will follow.

In an interview with *New York Times*, Marc Benioff, billionaire CEO of Salesforce, said, "This idea that somebody put into our heads—that companies are somehow these kind of individuated units that are separate from society and don't have to be paying attention to the communities they're in—that is incorrect."[3]

He went on to talk about the kind of impact he wants Salesforce to make on their local homeless community in San Francisco. From the very first day, he said he wants

---

3 https://www.nytimes.com/2018/06/15/business/marc-benioff-salesforce-corner-office.html

employees to feel they are receiving from the company so that they can then give to others. Speaking of service, he also said, "We cannot delegate these complex problems off to the government and say, 'We're not all part of it.'"

Clearly, Marc has learned a thing or two from his vast business experience. Namely, he has understood the importance of a company having a purpose that goes beyond profit.

YOUR COMPANY'S PURPOSE

In my opinion, if you're only building a business to earn money, you have a poor business. That might sound harsh, but I want to be honest with you. You are never going to meet your goal because it's never going to be enough. You're going to live month over month and quarter over quarter. I have known many people who run their companies this way. They think their purpose is to profit, but they don't have any true core driving force behind what they do.

Having said that, I am 100 percent someone who focuses on profit. We look at our finances every week to make sure we're making a profit. We are running a company, after all. You can't go to the bank that gave you a loan and say, "Sorry, we can't pay. We've got a purpose." That would be like going home to your spouse and saying, "I'm not making any money, but I have a purpose." It's not going to work out so well.

What I do believe is that there is a more enjoyable way to operate than to focus on profit. My happiest time isn't earning a dividend check or profit check as owner. My happiest time is hearing that someone got promoted. I will keep betting on genuine care and compassion.

If you choose to focus only on money, on quarter over quarter performance, the truth is that you will wind up spinning your wheels. A competitor could come in and change everything. Maybe it's a fight to the top. Maybe it's a fight to the bottom. Whatever the case, your focus on profit can never be your differentiator.

When I joined 1-800-GOT-JUNK? before the market crash in 2008, I saw that they had the right mentality. Yes, they suffered during the market crash, but once the market turned around, they were able to get back to where they had been, and they grew even more than when they started. They maintained the same principles through tough conditions and didn't change the way they operated. Their saying is, "It's all about people," and that didn't go away during tough times. They remained true to their core values, so when the market turned around, they became bigger than before the market crashed. Their People-First Culture, which was governed by their core purpose, was their differentiator.

FOCUSING ON OUR TWOFOLD PURPOSE

Our first purpose as a company is to help team members grow as leaders; it's core to everything we do. Because we have a People-First Culture, we're constantly seeking ways to invest in our team members. We don't take all of our profits. Instead, we reinvest them back into our team. When we open a new venue, many of the leaders from our first venue will move to the second. By investing in this team, we are set up for sustainable growth.

On the customer side, our sustainable growth comes from customer loyalty, which is why our secondary purpose is to provide guests with an excellent customer experience. I believe we have succeeded because we have the city of Toronto talking. People are coming back again and again, which has produced predictable, sustainable growth.

Other successful companies often have a similar purpose to value their employees and customers. How, for example, did Netflix beat Blockbuster? At Netflix, one of the core values is employee freedom, which gave their engineers the freedom to create the technology that customers loved and that ultimately put Blockbuster out of business. Their success began internally, with leaders valuing employee freedom and empowering team members to do great work.

Blockbuster's original mission was this: "At Blockbuster, we are committed to supporting the communities that our members and employees call home." At first glance, the mission sounds good, but what did it actually produce? What was this nebulous community the company was supporting? How were they supporting it? Why didn't they instead focus on supporting members and employees directly?

Regardless of market conditions, being all about people is a sustainable business model. As I told a friend of mine over coffee a few years ago, regardless of how crowded the market is, there's always room for a company that focuses on employees and customers. You might think, *Do we really need another law firm in town?* Absolutely! After all, not many law firms are known for building a great workplace and delivering a great experience to customers. There are opportunities in every industry.

A BIGGER PURPOSE

Many companies have developed a way to build their purpose around environmental and social concerns, and B Corporations are a great example. According to Forbes, there are actually 2,000 B Corporations. Included in the list are companies like Kickstarter and Patagonia. According to bcorporation.net, "A B Corp is to business what fair trade certification is to coffee or USDA organic certification is to milk. B Corps are for-profit companies certified by the nonprofit B Lab to meet rigorous standards of social and environmental purpose, accountability and transparency." The success of these companies reinforces the idea that while profit matters, purpose matters more.

Patagonia is a great example of a company that has always been clear on its purpose. You might think, *Oh, they're a huge brand. I can't relate.* It's important to remember they were once a small brand with the same exact purpose. Patagonia grew out of a small company that made tools for climbers. Since the beginning, it has valued the environment. Part of their mission statement is to "cause no unnecessary harm and use business to inspire and implement solutions to the environmental crisis."

The Beautiful People Company, based in South Korea, is another great example of a company with a clear outward focus in their purpose. This time, their outward focus is toward their employees. Of their 214 employees, eighty-nine of them have physical disabilities. They manufacture men's clothing, but their purpose goes beyond the clothing. They want to create a culture of inclusion where anybody can come and do great work.

I was first introduced to this company by a friend, and I was blown away. On the surface, they seem like any other clothing manufacturer. They compete on product and price, but their key differentiator is that they welcome everyone to do great work and build the company together. I love that.

Some business leaders choose to have a bigger purpose, even against the advice of others. For example, Audible's CEO made a decision that most "experts" have said would hurt his profit and ability to grow—he moved the company to Newark, New Jersey. Some believed he would lose 25 percent of his workforce, but he had a desire to serve this community and provide more jobs. Sticking to this greater purpose, the company has continued to thrive and has only done better financially after the move.

IDENTIFYING YOUR COMPANY'S PURPOSE

The process to identify your company's purpose is simple but also difficult. Ask, *What do you want your employees and customers to think and feel when they see your brand or logo?* The question isn't all that difficult, but coming to your answer is.

You might struggle finding a way to have consistency between your purpose for your business and your own life. I believe it's worth working toward a consistent answer.

As Howard Behar said, your values should be the same at home and at work. What are your personal values? How can they help you build values for your company, which will help you create a clear purpose?

I shared in Chapter 1 how I want people to feel safe with me, and that's the same thing I'll want people to feel when I'm eighty years old. Similarly, you have to think long term with your company. Ponder, *What do you want your company to be remembered for in a hundred years?* You can't be self-serving. If all you can come up with is, "I want people to think we're the best in the market," you have to dig deeper. Why do you want to be the best in the market?

Core to our company's purpose—what I want the company to be remembered for—is excellent customer experience built on trust. If a customer only goes out to eat once every two weeks, I want them to choose our location because they trust they'll have a great experience. I want them to have complete peace of mind with us. This is deeply connected to my personal purpose.

USING YOUR PURPOSE TO DRIVE YOUR COMPANY'S PURPOSE

Eric Spofford runs addiction recovery centers across the nation. I interviewed him because I was curious about why he started down this particular path. He said, "I never actually started out to build a big company. I started out to help people, never expecting it to turn into what it has."

In the late nineties, Eric got caught up in an addiction to prescription painkillers that then moved to heroin addiction. He shared with me how that addiction nearly took his life many times and caused him immeasurable pain and suffering for many years. After trying to turn his life around on multiple occasions, he finally got sober in 2006. Through that experience, he saw how important community was in the road to recovery. He started volunteering, running recovery workshops for those without insurance or money, and then figured out how to start his first sober living home. He did everything on his own at first, and other facilities came after that. Today, Granite Recovery Centers is recognized as a large brand with facilities across the Northeast of the United States.

Eric had his purpose long before the business. While he enjoys the money aspect of being an entrepreneur, he told me, "My happiness and how I experience my day-to-day can't ultimately come from how much money I make. It comes from my purpose."

Similarly, Peter "Flossy" Florentzos, who I mentioned in Chapter 1, has found a way to compete in a difficult industry by coming at real estate from a different angle and creating a unique company purpose out of his personal purpose—to enrich the lives of others. He told me, "If you look after people, money comes naturally. If you chase money, people don't come naturally. If you connect with people really deeply, then the decision to choose you is easier for the team member or customer. The key to our business is referrals and repeat customers, which is only achieved by truly caring and serving."

THE STARTING POINT

Finding your purpose is the starting point. If you want to earn profit, if you want to build something grand and be admired, if you want to beat your competition, first find a purpose. However you define success, you must start with your purpose; it's nonnegotiable.

As you've seen and will continue to see with the companies mentioned in this book, the proof is in the pudding. Purpose is where you must start, even if you've never operated this way before. It's okay to feel vulnerable. You might stumble a bit at first, but once you find that purpose and pursue it, your work will be so rewarding.

I have spent time on this part of the book because you must get your mentality right to be able to build a People-First Culture. Now, I can show you the mechanics of *how* to build and maintain this culture.

PART II

★ ★ ★ ★ ★

PROCESS: HOW TO IMPLEMENT A PEOPLE- FIRST CULTURE

CHAPTER 5

RECRUITING AND HIRING: WHERE MOST LEADERS GO WRONG

Now that you understand the importance of mindset, let's move on to the "how to," the step-by-step guide, which is where so many leaders go wrong. If your company is growing quickly, you need to have the right processes that allow everyone to adopt the ideas living in your head.

If I were to have a conversation with a leader right now, I would say, "You believe in this stuff? Great. If this isn't working for you, it's because you haven't documented the framework and built step-by-step guides so others in the organization can help you actually implement a People-First Culture. You can't be in the building 100 percent of the time. You need to infuse this culture into everything you do."

In my company, we have everything we do to implement this culture documented in nicely designed, colorful playbooks with graphics to make the concepts come to life and feel more real. If the information remains as bullet points in a document, it will never be important to you. However you need to make what I share in this part of the book come to life—invest the time to do it. Your investment will change your organization for the long run.

Before documenting, you need to actually build the processes and implement the systems that support your message. The culture will only be ingrained into the DNA of the company once you are taking daily action in alignment with it. Here, I'm going to give you the framework to build these processes. Each chapter is packed with useful tips and insights. Strap on your seat belts!

We begin with recruiting, a foundational part of building a People-First Culture. If you recruit well, you will also have cost savings that go straight to your bottom line.

RECRUITING DONE RIGHT

I have learned over time to stop using the term "human resources." Tucker Max, famed author and CEO of Scribe

Media, says it best when he says, "Coal is a resource. People are the point." How do we start to take action based on this reality? We start with approaching recruiting and hiring the right way.

Many companies are lazy when it comes to recruiting. They just go through the motions—they create a job description, post it online, then wait for a superstar candidate to come along. This approach does not work.

Think of it this way: if you want to date a great guy or girl, you know you can't simply go through the motions. You have to expend a bit of effort. You have to stand out and be unique. You have to take time to look for the right match, for someone who stands out from the rest. Anything good in life takes time, and it's no different with finding the right people for your company.

First, start internally. Before you post a job description on Indeed, buy a Facebook ad, or hire a recruiting firm, look at your current team. You likely have A-players in your team right now who might fit the role. In other cases, your team will recruit for you. When you are scaling, everyone on the team needs to actively participate in the recruiting process.

Think about it. When was the last time you shared a job description with your team and asked for input on who may best fit the role? Odds are it's been a while—or never. To encourage them to interact, you can incentivize your team, but you don't have to. People like working with friends and people they trust. A-players like to hang out with other A-players.

Using our internal team has worked so well for us that we no longer have to recruit externally. You might have happened to find new team members through your team by happenstance, but is this outlined as a first step in your recruiting playbook? Is everyone on board?

You could also leverage your relationship with your best customers, as long as it's a relationship built on trust. Send them the job description with a message like, "Do you know anyone who fits this role? I thought of you because you're so loyal to the brand." Whenever we're looking to fill a position, we send the job description to several regular customers. Maybe their niece needs a job as a hostess—you never know! We found our bar manager through a loyal customer, which saved us thousands in recruiting costs. We trust these people, and they trust us, so their recommendation can be a win-win.

Finally, you can ask your vendors to help. The company that sells us steaks has people working in kitchens every day, so they might know a great executive chef, sous chef, or chef de partie. Your own vendors could have the perfect connection to bring you the right fit.

THE EMPLOYEE MUSE

To enhance our recruiting efforts, we use what we call the "employee muse," a well-thought-out, one-page document describing our ideal candidate. The muse can aid you by painting a picture of the kind of person you need to recruit. Sure, you may have a general idea of who this person will be, but does everyone in the company share your thoughts? As mentioned, you should have an all-hands-on-deck approach to recruiting, especially while you're growing.

The employee muse can include descriptions of necessary qualities. For example, if you need someone who can work in an environment that is fast-paced and high stress, such as hospitality, you might include in the muse that this person knows how to take care of themselves by exercising or doing yoga.

EXAMPLE FOR OUR FACE OF HOUSE MUSE

Our Face of House team will consist of a mix of men and women who primarily live downtown with a look that shows their personality, energy, and commitment to self. Most will have previous experience from a recognizable restaurant that locals respect and recognize or a professional retail environment. We eagerly welcome people who understand how to sell and who understand how important the customer experience is to our success.

Alongside strong sales and customer experience skills comes culture fit—everyone we hire believes in what we are building and wants to be a part of our mission. We're looking for people who are driven by passion and are involved in activities outside of work in the arts, health and wellness, and community. They already (or aspire to) dine at some of Toronto's best restaurants and know what it takes to not only meet, but exceed guests' expectations.

They are career-minded individuals who are looking to Baro as their next great opportunity or a springboard to future opportunities that fulfill them. We want our team members to learn, contribute, and succeed, both professionally and personally.

THE SEARCH

Once we have the document in place, we go fishing. If you're going to fish for a particular type of person, you have to target the right body of water. Then, you need to know what will attract this kind of fish, where she or he swims, and so forth. I know this is a strange analogy, but that's how we think of the process of narrowing down our search.

I was inspired by lululemon, a company that uses a customer muse. When I first saw their model, I wondered if it could work for my company—and it does.

You can post the job description on Facebook, Indeed, and Monster, but you can't just sit and pray that someone good comes along. The reason I encourage looking internally first is because most A-players are already gainfully employed, so not many of them are actively looking for a job. Sometimes the only way to find that perfect person described in your customer muse is to use your internal relationships.

There are many A-players working for average companies, waiting for the right opportunity to present itself. In this case, it's your job to entice them and bring them into your company, and that's not going to happen by simply "spraying and praying." Your best chance to reach an A-player is through someone they trust, like a friend, family member, or neighbor. Cameron Herold, who is a friend of mine and former COO of 1-800-GOT-JUNK?, once said, "A leader's job is to build a great culture that becomes a magnet for great employees. Build your culture and make a compelling argument for people to leave their company for yours."

You can still use the traditional steps, of course. We still post job descriptions on LinkedIn and other websites, but first, we look internally. There are many benefits, including the fact that finding someone this way is more cost-effective. If you end up needing to only recruit 25 percent of the time, you will be left with more cash to give back to those who helped you recruit internally.

SEVEN-STEP INTERVIEW PROCESS

Now you have found a few potential candidates, and you need to interview to find people who will fit your culture. Other than what I shared in the dedication to my mother at the beginning of this book, I am most proud to share the following interview process with you. This process, above anything else, has allowed us to build a People-First Culture. It has earned us a retention rate two and a half times higher than industry average and saved us a ton of time and money in the long run.

The process was created over a two-year period and continues to evolve. For example, the questions we ask candidates during certain steps changes, so that candidates don't know what to expect, and so that those doing the interviews stay engaged.

Here is the seven-step interview process I use every time we need to hire someone new:

1. Phone interview
2. Predictive Index assessment
3. Culture interview
4. Skillset interview
5. Assignment
6. Decision
7. Offer

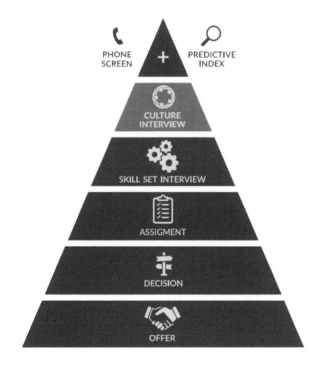

I came up with this process before we opened our flagship location. We had to hire ninety-seven people in forty-five days, and we didn't want to hire just anyone with a pulse. I thought, *This is a highly volatile industry with high turnover, so how can our interview process set us up for success from the start in building the right team?*

Whenever I speak, I get a lot of positive response about this process. People follow up with me, wondering how to implement it best in their company. Whether or not you use this exact process I outline here, you can learn from it and take what works for you. Though seven steps might sound like a lot, I have found that all of them help you find the perfect fit.

PHONE INTERVIEW

The first step is the phone screen. In this step, I pay attention to how the person answers the phone. Do they sound enthusiastic to hear from me? If I get their voicemail, what does their voicemail sound like?

If the person does not represent themselves well over the phone, what is the likelihood they will represent your brand well? At this stage, I look to filter out more people than continue on to the next step. Sound harsh? It is! The process must be a type of gauntlet. You must make it difficult for people to join the team, or you will be doing yourself, your team, and your brand a disservice.

PREDICTIVE INDEX

The next step is called the Predictive Index, which is a two-question behavioral assessment we give each prospect to complete, which ultimately tells us how we should manage them.

The two questions are as follows:

1. Please read the words in the list below and check those that you feel describe the way you are expected to act by others.
2. Continue by reading the words in the list below, now checking those that you yourself believe really describe you.

This list includes words like *bold*, *aware*, and *careful*. There are roughly ninety words to choose from.

My friend, Rob Friday, who is based in Toronto, is licensed as a Predictive Index professional. When I asked him why it works so well, he said, "This will give you a window into what it's going to be like working with that person six months down the road. With two questions, it shows you what really makes that person tick. It will help you answer the following questions: What kind of work are they going to find satisfying? What sort of growth opportunities are they going be interested in? Finally, does that all align with the opportunity you're providing to them?"

The Predictive Index is a "free choice" assessment. It has been around for over sixty years and is rooted in scientific validity. Practically, it helps you see a person's natural behavior and their adaptive behavior. It will allow you to see how you might use their natural strengths but also how they would be able to change.

Rob noted the biggest issue companies have with the Predictive Index is the transfer of knowledge. In other words, you can use it to hire great people, but you have to pass on the knowledge about these people based on their profiles so that others on your team know how to manage them properly. Otherwise, this step is useless.

CULTURE INTERVIEW

The third step is the culture interview. At this point, the candidate comes in to meet us in person. During this interview, we ask questions specifically related to company culture. Beyond their answers, we're also evaluating their behavior. The person could be the best cocktail artist in Toronto, but if they're an ass, they're not getting hired.

Note that we do the culture interview before we delve into skills, because we don't want to become enamored with a person's talents before finding out they're a jerk. I tell our management team not to bring the resume to the culture interview, meaning all they know is the person's name and the position they're applying for. I don't want the interviewer looking at their work experience until step four.

I recommend asking questions related to your company's values. In our company, we have five core values—celebration, ownership, foresight, humility, and integrity. We ask two questions related to each core value to measure how well the candidate will naturally adopt our culture. I love this prompt: "Intimately describe a time you planned a celebration. What was it like?" This is obviously connected to our first core value and shows us how well a candidate will know how to celebrate our guests and team members. I also always ask one unique question here: "What's an indulgence you can't live without that costs less than twenty dollars?" You'll see more about why I ask that question in the next chapter.

SKILLSET INTERVIEW

The fourth step is the skillset interview, which is conducted by different managers depending on the position. This interview is just what it sounds like. We are looking to see if the person can actually make a cocktail or cook. This interview would look different for each position.

At this stage, we also ask about a dozen questions specific to the role. Most companies already know how to do this part well. The problem is that this is often the only step in the interview process. Reed Hastings, CEO of Netflix, once said, "Do not tolerate brilliant jerks. The cost of teamwork is too high." Too many companies do not follow this advice. They hire only based on skillset. It's easy to focus on the fact that someone can do a job well. Seemingly, this will make your job easier. However, it's not that simple. We look for things like humility. Awesome! You can cook a great paella, but can you work as a team player? If not, it's not going to work out. Even in the skillset interview stage, we're still evaluating for culture fit.

As in the previous step, we ask a seemingly random question: "What is a non-work-related skill you want to develop over the next twelve months?" We might give examples like salsa dancing, learning to sky dive, or learning to speak Italian. We ask this question to get to know the person but also to plan ahead. You'll see how we utilize their answer in the next chapter.

ASSIGNMENT

In step five, we give the prospect an assignment based on the position they're applying for. If we're hiring a marketer, we might ask them to edit a full page of copy for grammar and diction. Then, we may ask them to tell us what we should be doing on a particular social media channel to improve our performance. If they're interviewing to be a bartender, we might ask them to make three cocktails on the spot with no advanced notice or preparation. These assignments mirror the real, everyday work these candidates would be doing, more so than the general skillset interview.

Whenever possible, I like giving take-home assignments, which I often send at 4:00 p.m. on Friday and request back by 10:00 a.m. on Monday. I do this on purpose. I want to see who's willing to give up some of their weekend to work for our company. If someone can't sacrifice their weekend to secure their career, what is the likelihood they are going to go above and beyond for your team, customers, and company? The people who don't return the assignment or return it half-finished aren't worth investing in. They're not taking the opportunity seriously.

DECISION

At this point, all of the interviewers who met with the candidate meet to decide. This step happens behind the scenes and should be done quickly so that the prospect isn't left hanging. At too many companies, prospects have to wait for weeks or months to know if they are hired. So many companies I have worked with never get back to non-hires. If the decision is to not continue on with someone, you should reach out to them as soon as you can. This is what admired companies do. If the decision is to hire, an offer needs to be made.

OFFER

The offer should be celebratory. At many companies, offers are made through email by a team member that the candidate never met. The email might say, *Congratulations, John. We look forward to having you. Please fill out these documents. See you on day one.* There's no emotion, even though a candidate might be relocating or leaving a job they've had for ten years. One of our core values is celebration. We celebrate each new hire, and we celebrate each other. This celebration builds the right culture from the start.

When making an offer, we have one of our hiring managers or our general manager call the candidate with at least two other people on a speaker phone. These others on the phone say, "Congratulations! You haven't met me yet. My name is Zoe. I work in the kitchen. You're probably going to see me here on Mondays and Tuesdays. I just wanted to say we're looking forward to having you. I've heard great things." By having multiple people introduce themselves and congratulate the new hire, they feel welcomed.

GROUP INTERVIEWS

In many cases, we also add a group interview as part of our process. If we're hiring hostesses, for example, we might conduct a group interview simply because we've received many candidates. We wouldn't do a group interview for a general manager position, on the other hand, because we usually don't have more than ten candidates.

Group interviews happen after a person has passed the phone screen and the Predictive Index. For these events, we'll contact the candidate and say, "Okay, Joey, on Wednesday at 10:00 a.m., there's going to be a group interview. There will be a number of other people gunning for this position around the same table, answering the same questions, along with one or two representatives from the company."

We always notify candidates they'll be walking into a group interview. We want them to know upfront to see how they come into the situation. Do they play nice? Do they try to sabotage others? Some people think they're being competitive, but they're actually being rude. We notice this behavior. If they're willing to act like that during the interview, what will they be like in the workplace? That won't work for a People-First Culture.

CANDIDATES DROPPING OUT

We often find many people drop out of our interview process around step four—and that's a good thing. You actually want people to drop out. I would go so far as to say the process is designed to squeeze people out, because it forces people to show their true colors and display how committed they are. There's no way a person will be committed to the brand if they can't commit to this process.

We spoke earlier about Jordan. He went through the most challenging interview process I've ever put anyone through. It began with fifty candidates, and only four made it as far as the assignment. Only two submitted the assignments, and he was one of them. Since then, he's become like my right-hand person for everything related to marketing and branding for our company.

He passed the interview process and truly gave himself to the company. He exemplified so many strengths during that process, and even though I felt kind of bad for putting him through it, the process allowed us to add a great person to the team. As mentioned earlier, he was promoted within a year to marketing manager, which is supporting his career goal of owning a digital marketing agency.

DON'T RUSH THE PROCESS

This recruiting, interviewing, and hiring process can change everything for your company. You will find people who truly want to be there. The hires you make will increase the quality of the work, the culture, and every other aspect of the company. Still, people often think this process sounds too long. Again, I return to the reality of personal relationships we build in life. We spend time auditing friends, don't we? We don't just let anyone into our lives. We even spend time considering who to invite to our wedding or Christmas party. Shouldn't we spend more time figuring out who to invite to be part of our company?

Does the process of recruiting and hiring require effort? Yes. Don't try to expedite the process. The worst thing you can do is add the wrong people to your team. That goes against everything I'm teaching in this book. Roll up your sleeves and do the work. Get your team involved. Leverage your current relationships—but, again, don't rush the process.

The processes I've shared in this chapter have worked for me for many years, and I've often had to hire many people in short periods of time. If you follow my advice, you will be able to front-load the work for the sake of employee retention. Have you calculated how much time, effort, and money you've spent because of low employee retention? That is the real cost. Again, I'm advocating a long-term approach to building the right culture.

This being said, the processes I've shared here aren't all drudgery. You can have fun with them. You can get to know new people and build a team that is just right.

CHAPTER 6

EMOTIONAL ONBOARDING: MAKING EMPLOYEES CRY

You've recruited well. You've saved some money because you were able to find people internally rather than externally. You took the candidates through a rigorous interview process, and they're excited to join your team. What happens now?

According to a survey given to hundreds of HR professionals, 53 percent say employee engagement rises when onboarding is improved.[4] Why, then, don't we spend time on this crucial step? When new team members show up for work, why do so many companies simply show them their desk and have them get to work? We ask them to

---

4   http://hr1.silkroad.com/state-of-talent-2017

deliver a great experience for customers, but why don't we deliver a great experience for them?

These new team members don't know anybody. The first week is often awkward for them. Many companies don't help by focusing only on the technical side of onboarding. I encourage you to consider how you are addressing the emotional needs of new hires right from their first day.

THE $20 QUESTION

During the culture interview, we ask people, "What is an indulgence you can't live without that costs less than $20?"

They might reply, "I'm a fiend for Ben & Jerry's ice cream."

"Okay, cool. What type of Ben & Jerry's ice cream?"

"Oh, I love the chocolate chip cookie dough."

Another person might say, "I love Skittles, but I only love the red ones."

We call this the $20 question. The candidate will wonder why you asked, but they'll quickly forget about it as you continue with the rest of the interview.

Why do we ask this question? What gift do you think is

waiting for that individual on their first day on the job, right at their workstation, with a handwritten card from the company owner? That same $20 indulgence they mentioned during the interview.

This simple step doesn't cost much money, but the candidate has likely never had that experience during onboarding. From the first day, their level of engagement increases. High engagement is critical during their first day's learning on the job, as it helps with retaining knowledge. Ultimately, that new team member will end up selling better, marketing better, and serving better right from the start—all from a simple $20 tactic.

When you bring someone new into your company, you are asking them to give themselves to the company, the customers, and the team. I believe that it is first essential to give yourself to them. This tactic shows your investment in them from the very start.

It also has an impact at home. When the candidate comes home with a box of Frosted Flakes, which was his onboarding gift, his wife will say, "Frosted Flakes? You bought that?" He can say, "No, you have to hear the story behind how I got these Frosted Flakes." You're making an impact in the home. We call this kind of positive word of mouth "owning the dinner table." It all begins with the emotional side of the onboarding process.

THE BUDDY SYSTEM

We also like to use the buddy system. If someone comes on board as a bartender, their buddy mentor for the first week might be a line cook. The "buddy" will never be their boss or someone in the same department. From the start, we want the new team member to start meeting people in other departments. Too often, employees don't meet anyone from other departments for weeks or even months, but we bridge that gap early. The buddy meets the new team member at the reception desk on day one so the new person doesn't feel awkward. Then, they show the new person around the building and introduce him or her to everyone.

Emotional onboarding is all about designing what employees see, feel, and hear during their first month of employment. What they see is the education material, which we'll discuss in the next chapter. What they feel is the $20 gift, the emotional aspect. What they hear is how they are welcomed into the company. Are people hospitable? Do they introduce themselves to the new team member? We want new people to feel a sense of camaraderie on day one, fully embraced into the culture.

THE ONE-YEAR GIFT

Though I've never made somebody cry over the $20 gift we give them, I have made them cry over their first-year gift. Again, this is all about emotional impact. Though this isn't technically part of onboarding, it's a continuation of the same philosophy.

During the skillset interview, we also ask, "What is a non-work-related skillset or experience that you want to have in the next twelve months?" They might say they want to skydive or learn how to Salsa dance. They might say they want to learn how to speak Italian because their grandmother in Italy can't speak English. The opportunities are endless.

On the one-year anniversary of their tenure with the company, we buy them whatever they mentioned during that interview before they were hired. If they wanted to learn Italian, we might pay for a year's subscription to high-end online software. We might also pay for software that enables them to speak to their grandmother in Italy. We once sent someone to Columbia to visit her grandmother whom she hadn't seen in years. These are the kinds of things that tug at the heartstrings.

I say, "I want employees to cry," in a good way. When someone arrives on the first day and realizes we care about them, they get an immediate taste of our People-First Culture. I wouldn't be surprised if more of our new team members go home after their first day and cry. Many people haven't ever experienced anything like this when it comes to their jobs.

EMBRACING EMOTIONAL ONBOARDING

Of course, emotional onboarding isn't simply about making employees sappy. As I mentioned, it truly increases engagement. With a high level of engagement, new team members are naturally motivated to serve customers and do their job well.

If you are a leader who is willing to serve your team in an emotional way, you'll soon realize that your job isn't as difficult as you thought. You are presenting a workplace people have never seen before, and that is all you need to do. You can then get out of the way, as your team will gladly do the work on your behalf.

Why don't more companies adopt the emotional side of onboarding? I don't think they realize the value of it. They see it as fluffy stuff. These companies might hear the idea of the $20 gift and blow it off as childish. If they were willing to embrace emotional onboarding and present the gift with genuine care, they would realize how much a little gesture can mean.

If you think these ideas are interesting but don't think they would work for you and your company, I would politely suggest you're wrong. You might have reservations about them because you're not the one who should be doing them; that doesn't mean you should throw them out the window. If you can't be the creative, engaging person, don't force yourself to play that role. It will come across as inauthentic or awkward. Find the right leader to lead this cause. Find someone you can partner with who can be the flag bearer for emotional onboarding.

EXAMPLES ABOUND

You don't have to just take my word for the effectiveness of emotional onboarding. There are many companies that get onboarding right. Remember Eric Spofford, the entrepreneur I introduced in the first part of the book who runs addiction recovery centers across the country? He emphasizes the importance of new team members embracing the culture right from the start. He often has a one-on-one sit down with new hires to get to know them. He also wants them to know he will be keeping up with them. "A handshake and high five or a ten-minute conversation go a long way," he told me. He has built emotional onboarding around these simple upfront engagements, making new people feel welcome.

In his case, many new hires are people whose lives were literally saved by the recovery programs. Because of this life-changing experience, they have no problem adopting the mission and carrying on the purpose for others. Even though engagement happens almost automatically, Eric still believes in making sure new team members know they are important and seen.

There are more examples. When a new employee starts at Warby Parker, the eyewear company, they get a welcome package. It includes two pairs of glasses: one for the employee and one for a family member or friend. It also includes a gift certificate to have their eyes examined and a bag of Martin's Pretzels. Why do they include the pretzels? For no other reason than because one of the founders of the company really likes Martin's Pretzels. He found himself eating them frequently when they were starting the company, so they throw in a bag.

They also throw in a $100 gift certificate to a Thai restaurant. Why? Because when the founders of the company were getting started, they had many late nights, and there was a Thai restaurant around the corner from the office that was open past midnight.

Lastly, they include a book called *Dharma Bums*. When they were trying to figure out the name of the company, they got stuck. They had a thousand possible names, and one of the founders was reading *Dharma Bums*. In the book, one of the characters is named Warby, and another character is named Parker, so the founder said, "Why don't we name the company Warby Parker?" It worked.

Sharing these kinds of startup stories is a great way to help new employees live the early days of the company without having been there. When new people hear the stories, they feel part of something bigger and want to tell others, too.

Take Bonobos, for example. They do something during the interview process called "two truths and a lie." The candidate is asked to share two things that are true about them and one that isn't. If that person is hired, their People Department will send an email to the whole company that says, "Hey everyone, Joey and Samantha are starting today. Here are Joey's two truths and a lie, and here are Samantha's. The first person to figure out which ones are true and which ones are a lie for both employees will get a fifty-dollar gift certificate to purchase clothing from our website."

Picture that! On day one, multiple employees are approaching the new team members and talking to them, trying to figure out which facts are true and which are lies. It's a simple but creative way to break the ice, and it helps new employees feel connected and engaged—crucial in developing a People-First Culture.

CHAPTER 7

LEARNING AND DEVELOPMENT: HELPING EMPLOYEES TAKE ACTION

To continue to raise engagement levels, team members need to be equipped to take action. In this chapter, we'll explore why some companies create remarkable learning programs and others don't. I will share ways you can give your team members, regardless of their department, the right education to be able to serve.

You might have noticed that I don't use the word "train" or "training" in this book. Instead, I use the words learning, development, and education. I was motivated to change my language in this area by a great business leader, JT

McCormick, who doesn't use the word "training" when speaking of employees.

In an article he shared on LinkedIn, he wrote, "We don't train people. That's condescending and dehumanizing. You train dogs, horses and dolphins. If I say I'm training someone, it doesn't inspire them to be better. But if I take my time to teach them, to coach them, and possibly even mentor them—that excites them and makes them want to be involved. Because it's about them. Training is about me."[5]

With this simple change in my own language and thinking, I was able to better implement this step of developing a People-First Culture.

Whether team members are in traditional customer service, sales, or a non-customer-facing department, everyone should get the same level of education. Whether they speak to a hundred customers a day or to one, everyone needs to be on the same page. This way, anybody who interacts with your brand will get the same level of service, whether they are a customer, media, vendor, business partner, or someone who got lost and is simply asking for directions.

---

5   https://www.linkedin.com/feed/update/urn:li:activity:6431158250519044096/

INVEST IN EDUCATION

Too often, companies half-ass their learning programs. Your programs need to be robust and make a real difference. What has helped the Starbucks brand become a household name? Howard Schultz, former CEO of Starbucks, believes the answer is education. He said, "Everybody thinks Starbucks is a great advertising company, but we actually don't advertise at all. We take what the traditional company would spend on advertising, and we spend it on education." Think about that. When was the last time you saw a Starbucks commercial? Never!

Why are so many companies quick to invest in traditional marketing tactics but slow to invest in education? In our personal lives, we readily spend money on children's, even our own, learning and development. Again, we need to learn to operate in our businesses the way we operate in our personal lives.

If you say you're invested in your employees and customers, I want you to show me your robust learning and development program. Do you cut corners when it comes to learning and development? Show me the investments you make in your people. Show me the budget you have for learning and development each quarter.

Many business leaders view education the wrong way. They think of it as an expense rather than an investment in growing their team and, ultimately, their customer base. If you don't invest in educating your people, I can ensure you that you will pay for it down the road.

The return on investment for all the time, money, and resources you spend on education doesn't always show up right away. If I educate my team today, I don't necessarily see the fruits of that labor tomorrow. As in many other areas of the business, we look at our development initiatives with a long-term mindset, knowing that if we invest in a team member's education, they're going to serve the company well for years to come. Some business leaders don't have enough patience for this kind of long-term investment, so they keep running marketing campaigns that give them results right away. The problem is that a marketing campaign won't ensure your brand will stay strong for a hundred years; a strong team that has been invested in it will.

Finally, I want to challenge you to consider how you are viewing your team. Do you view your employees as subordinates? If so, you will never understand the importance of investing into their lives. I see executives and senior management teams investing in themselves through executive retreats and so forth, but the frontline employees—those who speak to customers more than the executive team—get the short end of the stick. This doesn't work in a People-First Culture.

REINVIGORATING AN ORGANIZATION THROUGH DEVELOPMENT

Lawyer Trane is an HVAC company based in Las Vegas that's been around for forty years. They do the majority of the HVAC work for all the major hotels in Las Vegas. The company is still owned by one person—Tom Lawyer, the founder. A couple years ago, he brought me in to help them build a people-centric company.

HVAC companies aren't particularly known for being people-first, like a hospitality company might be. Tom Lawyer and his team wanted to be different. Even as a company that, at various points, was named one of *Inc.* Magazine's Fastest Growing Companies and had been recognized as the Best Service Company in the state of Nevada, the leaders understood the value behind continually developing their people.

When I recently interviewed Tom, he explained that things really changed for them when they had a single point of accountability, or the ambassador, for their customer experience, employee engagement, and company culture efforts. Initially, that person was me, until the role could be handed off to someone else on the team who was equipped to be the new flag bearer. In the end, the entire team felt equipped to meet customers more effectively and to stand out as a business by being people-first. Their investment into education and development reinvigorated their entire organization.

WHAT TO INCLUDE

Regardless of what you sell, what service you provide, or how big your company is, there are a few components I believe every education program should include to empower your team members with clear ways to act. Sometimes, it's helpful to have sources outside the organization help to educate your team in the following ways.

- Education on the difference between customer service and customer experience. Customer service is about the actions you take. Customer experience is the combination of macro and micro interactions your customers have while doing business with you from beginning to end. Going to the movie theater can work as an example. On the surface, the points of interactions are when you buy your tickets, arrive at the movie theatre, go to the concession stand, enter the theater. However, other smaller interactions include parking, going to the bathroom, getting ketchup or mustard. At each of these points, your team should know how to provide excellent customer service. In the end, great customer service at each point of interaction leads to a great customer experience.
- Education on how to identify the three customer per-

sonality types (director, socializer, passive), which we discussed earlier in the book.

- Education on the importance of organic growth, which is the revenue earned through repeat customers and word-of-mouth marketing. Organic growth is powered by team members in all departments. Everyone needs to know what it is and how they play a role. Your director of finance isn't customer-facing like a retail employee is. However, he or she still interacts with business vendors, partners, and financial institutions and therefore plays an important role in growing the business organically.
- Education on how to build and read customer journey maps, which are visual representations of every experience your customers have with you. These help to tell the story of a customer's experience with your brand from original engagement and into a long-term relationship.
- Education on how to achieve "service endurance," which is the ability to deliver the same high-level of service to the hundredth customer of the day as they did the first.

CUSTOMER INTELLIGENCE

Many companies teach their employees to listen to their customers. While listening is important, I tell our team that listening is a cheap skillset. You need to listen, but then you need to act on what you've heard to be truly people-first. In short, I want them to use *customer intelligence.*

If one of our customers indicates they've come to Baro to celebrate a recent pregnancy, we have a process in place where our servers and bartenders who capture that information will go straight to a manager and inform them. The manager will then use the budget to purchase a relevant gift. If someone is at our restaurant for a birthday, a pregnancy announcement, a recent graduation, or because they're visiting from out of town, we listen and act. Any company can, and should, listen and act in their own way.

Whether you capture information about a customer in person, over the phone, or via email, you can use it to improve the customer experience. For customer intelligence to be useful, your employees need to be taught how to respond quickly and effectively.

STAYING UP TO DATE

I know of a big company that had an extremely outdated training program. The core of the issue was that they didn't value their employees and therefore didn't want to invest in their development. How you stay up-to-date with development initiatives will say a lot about how you see your employees.

Just as we want to serve our customers well, we also want to serve team members by providing them with new, relevant content that will be interesting and useful to them. Just like students in school need up-to-date curriculum, team members need current content as well.

We also make sure our team members have access to the latest digital content instead of paper-based material. I recommend using learning management software so employees are better able to absorb their new learning. With greater knowledge retention, your team will be better equipped to implement what they've learned to serve customers. Customer experience, after all, begins and ends with your team.

CHAPTER 8

CUSTOMER EXPERIENCE: OWNING THE DINNER TABLE

So far, we've created a purpose, hired the right team, onboarded them correctly, and invested into them. Now, it's time to start focusing on our customer experience.

To get here, we had to first lay the foundation for our team—people who are committed to our purpose, our company, to themselves, and each other. Why? Because you can't ask somebody to take care of somebody else on your behalf if you haven't taken care of them first. That's why we focus on our inward strategy before trying to serve people outwardly, whether customers, vendors, or media.

Of course, you can be successful without a consistent outward focus. A big part of "people" in people-first is the customers you will serve. Even The Rock, named Forbes' highest-paid actor in the history of the Forbes' Celebrity 100 list and who earns $124 million equates his own success to this outward focus. On Instagram recently, he said, "I ALWAYS put my audience first." He even used the hashtag #AudienceFirstPhilosophy. Looks like we're on the same wavelength here. Now, where do I collect my $124 million?

As you develop great customer experience, you will need a mindset that is creative and flexible so you can figure out what people want in any given context. Everything is going to change five years from now, and customers will want different things. This chapter is a launching pad for ideas, but the core of customer experience is about serving the customer in such a way that they'll remember you and tell others about you.

With this kind of customer experience, you will "own the dinner table." In other words, your business will grow organically through word of mouth. To create that positive word of mouth, you'll need to create stories worth telling, which is where we'll begin.

MICRO CUSTOMER EXPERIENCES

We recently had a group of four ladies come into our

restaurant to celebrate a pregnancy announcement. Our server, Yasmin, heard what was happening and acted. She went to the manager on duty and let her know, and the manager used the information to create a micro customer experience. She went across the street to a local pharmacy and bought a $25 gift certificate for Toys"R"Us (before they filed for bankruptcy). She brought it back, and Yasmin wrote a note: *To you, your family, and baby. Congratulations!*

At billing time, we presented this small gift to the customer, and she was extraordinarily appreciative. Not only did she have a story to tell, but she also wrote a positive review on Facebook and Google. It's safe to say this woman and her friends will be customers for life. They will always remember this interaction, and they will all have a story worth telling at the dinner table. An added benefit was that our team members loved this micro customer experience too. They had a story to tell when they got home.

You can create more and more meaningful micro customer experiences by gamifying the process for your team members. For example, we actually host competitions in which team members who create the most memorable micro customer experiences win a gift certificate to our restaurant or a cash prize. We post the winners to our private Facebook group with shout out messages and photos.

Then, other team members can post their comments and messages of congratulation, too.

I encourage team members to "get into our guests' home or workplace" through the gifts they give. This kind of gifting is a form of marketing. Guests will remember the gesture for years to come, which builds a recurring brand impression.

Allowing space for micro customer experiences will require some financial investment, but it's worth it. In our case, we need an operational budget to purchase those small gifts for customers. Still, you can set whatever limit works for you. At our flagship location, which does ten million dollars a year in sales, our budget for customer gifts is only a few hundred dollars a month. We could afford more, but we make the budget lean. If our team knows it's lean, they will compete over it.

Conversely, if we had a big budget for micro customer experiences, team members would be handing out bottles of Dom Perignon to every customer, but the experiences wouldn't be memorable. We say "micro" because these experiences should purposefully be small, affordable, and memorable. A small gesture shows that you listened and retained some customer information just enough to provide a personalized gift.

Keep in mind you don't want gestures to be ones your

competitors could easily do as well. Giving flowers, for example, isn't that memorable. Plenty of people have received flowers before. It's easy to replicate. If you listen and take action on what you've heard, you can come up with a personalized gesture for a guest that they will remember. The point is not the price. The point is the experience.

You can't put a real value on micro customer experiences because you never know who an individual customer is. At Baro, we have people visit us from outside the country because they've heard about us. Even with these tourists, we'll still seek to provide a unique experience. One of them might share the story on Facebook or tell their friends to visit when they travel. In each unique case, our goal is to own the dinner table through recommendations and referrals.

THE ULTIMATE OUTCOME

Micro experiences are one lens through which you can see the importance of serving customers. Serving customers helps you grow. It helps you build a company that is admired in a way other companies are not. Remember, customer service at different points creates an overall customer experience. But service through micro experiences doesn't have to require large time investments. Once your team is familiar with the process, each micro experience can be accomplished in no time.

When you put customer experience front and center in your company, your team members will constantly want to exceed customer expectation. Seeing a customer have an amazing experience is addictive, and team members will continue looking for ways to outdo what has already been done. In this kind of workplace, there is no such thing as checking in and checking out. Everyone will feel a real desire to be part of what is happening.

LEARNING FROM OTHERS

I developed the concept of micro customer experiences in my own business based on strategies I learned from other business owners and companies. I love studying others who are successful, and I encourage you to do the same. You will find some common trends, especially when it comes to customer experience.

Marc Burrows and Peter Joudaki, friends and successful realtors at Progressive Real Estate based in Vancouver, told me a story that helped me see customer experience in a completely new way. One day, they were showing a couple a home in Vancouver, and the wife said, "Sweetheart, we haven't been to Victoria in a long time." (Victoria is an island off the coast that people from Vancouver often visit for vacation.)

Marc and Peter made note of this customer's comment.

They also overheard that the husband liked Italian food, and he noted that, too. After helping a couple buy the home, it's customary in the industry for realtors to purchase a gift for the new homeowners. Most of the time, this gift is a bouquet of flowers, though some realtors might buy a gift basket of wine and cheese or even a new TV for the home—great gifts, but not very creative.

Marc and Peter decided to do something different for this couple. They paid for a one-night stay at a nice hotel in Victoria and a ferry ticket for their car to get from Vancouver to their destination. They even found a great Italian restaurant in Victoria and set them up for dinner. They hand-delivered this gift to them. In a note, they wrote, "As we were building our relationship, you said a couple of things in passing that we made note of. Thanks for being our customer, and we hope you'll think of us if there's ever an opportunity to work together in the future or if you have family members or friends who are in the market for a home."

Through this amazing gift, they created a string of stories for these customers. This couple wouldn't only remember Marc and Peter, but they would certainly share their service with others if the opportunity to do so ever arose.

WARBY PARKER'S EXAMPLE

I first learned about micro customer experiences a few

years ago when I came across an article that blew me away. The article told the story of a customer who had ordered a pair of glasses from Warby Parker in Atlanta. When she went to pick them up, the employee asked, "How's your day going?" The customer replied, "Not well. I had my car stolen last night. I could really use a beer, but I'm excited to pick up my glasses."

The employee helped the customer but then went a step further, sending the customer a handwritten card that said, *Hey Tess! We were sorry to hear about your car. Since you won't be the designated driver anytime soon, here's a round on us! Love, your friends at Warby Parker. P.S. Your Durand frames look amazing!* The note included a $25 gift certificate to a local microbrewery so the customer could get the beer she wanted.

Naturally, this customer would have been inclined to share her great experience with friends. But little did she or Warby Parker know that *Mashable*, *Business Insider*, and *Huffington Post*, three websites that get tens of millions of views a month, would all write about this interaction. Talk about free marketing! If you track it back to the source, the story took place because the company put its people first. It hired correctly and encouraged its employees to truly care about customers. It created space for these micro customer experiences to happen.

CHAPTER 9

CUSTOMER ACQUISITION: USING CUSTOMER FEEDBACK

Do you understand why your customers are loyal to you? That might seem like a strange question to ask when we're talking about customer acquisition, but I believe customer loyalty and customer acquisition are directly aligned.

If you know why your customers love doing business with you, you will know how to acquire new customers. The entire process must be informed by your People-First Culture.

THE RIGHT WAY TO ACQUIRE CUSTOMERS

Every company since the beginning of time has wanted to

acquire new customers, but many only know how to get new customers in a transactional manner. In other words, once they sell the customer, the relationship is over. In essence, these companies say to new customers, "I got you through the door. Great. See you around."

As a customer, you might have had the experience of buying a product or service from a company that wined and dined you, put their best foot forward, and then never engaged you again. I won't name names, but software companies are notorious for taking this route. They exhaust a ton of effort upfront, do a great song and dance to get you to buy their product, and you never hear from them again.

To know how to acquire customers the right way, you simply need to know the right way to interact with humans. Do you really care about these people, or is it all just a show? Companies spend billions on marketing, and the amount they spend on customer experience pales in comparison. This makes no sense at all. If you aren't going to treat your customers right, why get them at all? You might convert a few people, but the lack of genuine human care and connection will ultimately come back to haunt you.

FEEDBACK

Now that we are aligned with the right way of looking at

customer acquisition, let's consider methods to do it well. If you have good feedback, you can leverage it to acquire new customers in an authentic way. Of course, you'll have to have feedback in the first place, which means you'll need to ask for it from your customers.

How do you solicit customer feedback in your company? Do you use the Net Promoter Score (NPS) or another customer satisfaction survey? Are you tracking your customer lifetime value? Personally, I like the Net Promoter Score survey. It's easy for customers, and they only have to answer two questions. It's also easy for your team to understand the score. The survey includes the following questions:

1. On a scale from 0-10, where 0 is absolutely not and 10 is absolutely, how likely are you to recommend [our company] to a family member or friend?
2. Based on your first response, what did we do or didn't we do to earn your score?

There are many naysayers for customer surveys like Net Promoter Score and Customer Effort Score, but I say forget the noise. Use whatever works best for your company, and when it stops working, look for something else.

The key is that you get the feedback in the first place. When you go through it, you can then take action. First, feedback helps you understand why customers don't do business with you again. Having this information will help you acquire and also retain more customers. You can know what needs to change. Even more importantly, feedback will reveal why customers do business with you.

THE TOP THREE REASONS

With my management team, my rule of thumb is that we need to know the top three reasons why our customers love doing business with us. If our current customers love us for these reasons, then prospective customers will love us for the same reasons. Now, all we have to do is figure out how to get in front of those prospective customers. You can take the top three reasons your current customers love you and put it into your marketing collateral, digital ads, and any other channels you use to acquire customers.

If the Alfa Romeo dealership down the street has customer loyalty because of friendly team members, competitive pricing, and a great location, then sales people need to use that language in their sales presentations. This same technique can be used whether you sell food, alcohol, photocopy machines, or anything else.

LOOK AT THE LANGUAGE

As you review feedback, you need to look at the exact

language being used. The top three reasons why we have customers who rate us highly on the Net Promoter Score is food quality, our level of customer service, and our ambiance (which includes décor, music, and our environment).

We give that information to our marketing team and ask them to create digital ads that speak to those three strengths—our food, our level of customer service, and our ambience. We tell our marketing team that if current customers are saying they love us for these reasons, then prospective customers will love us for these same reasons, too. We also ask customers' permission to use their testimonials on our website and in digital ads to extend the use of that exact language.

MANAGING NEGATIVE FEEDBACK

Feedback isn't always positive, and that's part of doing business. When a customer complains, having the right mentality goes a long way. You can think, *This is an opportunity to save a customer and learn something about our business so we don't make the same mistake again.* I like to think of "managing" negative feedback, rather than "dealing with" it. Again, little changes in our language can go a long way in changing our thinking.

Regardless of where a complaint or negative feedback comes from—whether via email, phone, social media, or in person—you need a process in place to deal with it. I refer to this process as the complaint resolution system, and it allows you to resolve all customer complaints across all platforms within one business day at most.

To start, you need a single point of accountability—one person in your business who is responsible for managing customer complaints. In a larger organization, it might be multiple people, or it might even be a whole department. For these people to be successful, they need the right education, the autonomy to make decisions, and the budget to be able to reimburse customers or give them a discount on future products or services. They also need to be celebrated. Working in the complaint resolution team of a company can feel like purgatory, so these team members need to be celebrated as ambassadors of the company. They are the last line of defense for your company.

Resolving a complaint is the easiest part. It's like putting out the fire. What is more difficult is getting to the root of why these complaints are happening in the first place so that you can truly restore customer confidence. If you can get to the root, you'll have a better understanding of what your next move should be. This move could ultimately help you get better feedback and also acquire more customers.

For example, at Baro, we had a complaint from customers

who said it was too hard to reach us when they called in. Rather than go into solution mode as soon as we received the first complaint, we observed a few complaints and decided it was something we needed to investigate. We audited our system. First, we called in ourselves. Then we had friends and family call in and document the experience. Since then, we've hired another part-time individual to answer calls during peak hours, and we also changed our phone system. We no longer use a phone tree, which gives the caller options: "Dial 1 for X or 2 for Y." Instead of making them jump through hoops, we simply answer the phone.

By responding to a negative feedback, we actually increased our opportunity to acquire new customers and set ourselves up to retain more customers, too.

CHAPTER 10

CUSTOMER RETENTION: RESPONDING TO CUSTOMER FEEDBACK

Customer retention is so important because it's not just about brand protection—it's also about customer loyalty. When a complaint is resolved in an effective manner, that customer will become more loyal to the brand than a customer who never had anything go wrong. Why? Because the customer was able to see the company show its true colors during a time of turbulence.

I *want* my company to receive complaints, and I think all entrepreneurs should want the same. That might sound ridiculous, but you show the authenticity of your brand during turbulent times. Whether a loyal customer complains, or a one-time customer complains, complaints keep you and your team humble and on your toes.

This is not about living from a place of fear. In actuality, you live in a place of fear when you are scared for any complaints to come your way. Instead of living in a place of fear, you can say, "I'm not afraid to receive complaints because I know they are actually good for us."

A HEALTHY FEEDBACK MANAGEMENT PROCESS

As I mentioned before, you need to have a single point of accountability, someone (or a department) who keeps track of customer complaints. Any complaint goes directly to this person or this team, and they have certain procedures and rules they follow to address it. They should also have a budget and the autonomy to respond.

You should also have a service-level agreement, which means all complaints are resolved within one business day, twelve business hours, one hour—depending on how good you can get. This agreement should never be for longer than one business day, but it should always be improving. Are you resolving complaints in a day? Great! Time to get down to twelve hours.

Receiving a complaint and responding by simply saying, "We're sorry for the bad experience" will only take you so far with some customers. Even if you have to pay up, don't see it as a loss. If you view this long term, you will see complaint resolution as an investment in securing that customer relationship. Not only do you secure that customer through your response, but you own the dinner table, because you're making sure they don't spread negative word of mouth.

L.A.S.T.

LAST stands for Listen, Accept, Sympathize, Take Action. It's a step-by-step process my management team came up with so our team members know exactly how to resolve complaints.

First, you need to listen and accept what you're hearing from the customer. Sometimes, what you hear is going to offend you, especially if you're the business owner. After all, you have a lot of pride in your business. *How could this happen to my business?* you might think. *This customer must be wrong.* While you need to do your due diligence, you should never become defensive in the moment they are explaining their issue to you. Next, sympathize with the customer, even if you're offended. Try to understand where they are coming from. Finally, take action. Do something. You don't have to give them exactly what they want, but you do need to respond.

At Baro, we've had experiences where a customer filed a complaint, so we listened to them, accepted what they said, and sympathized with them. However, upon further review, we realized the customer was trying to cheat us in what they were asking for. In those instances, we don't give them specifically what they ask for. Instead, we might say, "Mrs. Johnson, we listened to the call recording of your reservation. You specifically asked for Saturday in the call, not Sunday. We're very sorry. Here's a gift certificate for your next visit, but we can't give you the $1,000 reimbursement you're asking for because we did what you asked us to do."

An important reminder here is that I don't believe the customer is always right. Sometimes customers are malicious, and other times, they simply made a mistake. Still, they deserve to be heard and responded to. If this mentality is part of your People-First Culture no matter what, people will notice. Ultimately, your retention will increase as a result.

WHEN WE MESS UP

No company is perfect. What matters is how you respond when you mess up. For example, we once messed up big time with a Friday night reservation for eight people. The person who took the reservation booked it for the wrong Friday evening, and neither party (the guest or our team) noticed that the date was incorrect when the email confirmation was sent out.

To make matters worse, this reservation was for an engagement party, and one of the guests in the party had been recommended to come to Baro by a close friend from the LA Times. The LA Times rents out our building for the Toronto International Film Festival (TIFF) and is one of our biggest customers during one of the busiest times of the year in Toronto.

When the guests arrived and were informed that their reservation was not for that particular Friday, they were shocked and upset. Luckily, I was there that night with some friends, and was able to move, so the group could have our spot. Responding to major mess-ups is not always so easy, but one way or another, finding an effective response is worth it.

PART III

★ ★ ★ ★ ★

PROFIT: THE RESULT OF A PEOPLE-FIRST CULTURE

CHAPTER 11

THE ECONOMICS

Brian Chesky, cofounder and CEO of Airbnb, once wrote a letter to his entire team expressing the importance of culture. He shared it for the whole world to see in a Medium post.[6] In this letter, he explains how Peter Thiel, who had invested $150M in the company, had given him and his two partners one single piece of advice: "Don't fuck up the culture."

In this letter, Brian shared important insight that I would like to emphasize here. He wrote, "The thing that will endure for 100 years, the way it has for most 100-year companies, is the culture. The culture is what creates the foundation for all future innovation." At the end of the letter, Brian explained that he understands the pressures of growth and the need to ship new products. He wrote, "These problems will come and go. But culture is forever."

6 https://medium.com/@bchesky/dont-fuck-up-the-culture-597cde9ee9d4

And there it is. Ultimately, the economics of your business are directly aligned with the strength of your culture. Economics are the result. Peter Thiel understood this. Brian Chesky understands this. Do you?

DON'T BEGIN HERE

Many people begin right here with the economics—don't. Let me reiterate that profit comes last. It's important, but it must come last. It is the result. I absolutely believe in growing profitable companies, but my way of going about it is different.

I believe the mindset and processes I've shown you in this book will allow you to grow a profitable business, both relatively quickly and sustainably, so you don't have to worry quarter by quarter. Now that you have pursued excellence and built a People-First Culture, you can grow a business that is protected from disruption, competitors, and market conditions that you can't control.

In Part One, we talked about adopting the right mindset. In Part Two, we talked about getting your operations right. Now, we will look at the outcomes this people-first approach produces.

Do you remember my celebratory value? I have to say congratulations on getting to this point! You've gotten your mind right, and you're prepared to build some great systems. Now, you can reap the benefits.

ORGANIC GROWTH

Are you wondering what profit you are going to earn if you embrace a People-First Culture?

Consider, for a moment, the success of Southwest Airlines, a company that clearly displays a People-First Culture. Southwest has been profitable quarter over quarter, in an industry that is largely known for bankruptcy.

Baro itself isn't in an "easy" industry. When I tell people about what I do, they often look at me sideways and say, "Why would you get into hospitality? Can you even make money doing that?" The answer is yes, of course. You can make a lot of money in this industry if you pursue a People-First Culture and put the right systems and processes in place.

In any industry, you can create organic growth with a People-First Culture. When you have customers coming back and telling others about you, you have predictable revenue. I have known many companies that don't treat customers and employees well, and they also don't enjoy the luxury of predictable revenue. They are forced to live quarter by quarter. Quite frankly, I would hate to operate that way. It seems very stressful.

CUSTOMER LOYALTY AND TRUST

In 1994, Amazon started out of a garage in Seattle, Washington. At that time, they were almost certainly smaller than your business, so how did they grow into such a massive and highly profitable company? They began by building trust with their customer base, selling one product—books. When they realized customers trusted them, they began selling other products. As customer confidence grew, they moved into different verticals and industries. This ability to move to different verticals and take customers with them was the economic outcome of their People-First Culture.

I don't believe a company has earned the right to cross-sell or upsell their customers until they've built trust first, and that's exactly what Amazon did. They started with one product in very humble beginnings, and they focused. Eventually, the market allowed them to sell other products, and they had earned the right to do so. They haven't stopped earning the trust of their customers, and look at them now.

Amazon's slogan was never to have the largest website or become the biggest retailer. Their slogan, from day one until today, was "to be the world's most customer-centric company," a slogan that aligns perfectly with a People-First Culture. They've had the same people-first mentality since the days when they were operating out of a garage.

Nobody can dispute Amazon's success. Regardless of the size of your company today, you can learn from their example.

WAYS TO PROFIT

Putting people first increases the bottom line, though not in the way people think. Earlier, I shared a story about Warby Parker. Their kind gesture to a customer profited them from a branding perspective when websites like *Business Insider* and *The Huffington Post* wrote about them. Most companies have to pay PR agencies tens of thousands of dollars to get their stories told in such publications. Warby Parker did it through their People-First Culture—having a clear purpose in place and executing against it.

From a branding perspective, companies can profit from the word of mouth driven by a People-First Culture. From an employee perspective, this culture creates high employee retention, so companies don't have to recruit as much or hire as many recruitment firms.

FARHAN LALANI

Farhan Lalani, the CEO of Market One Media Group, who I introduced you to in the first part of the book, understands both sides of the money equation as a business owner.

In my interview with him, he told me why he believes most people aren't willing to move to a People-First Culture. "When you have a business that's spitting out cash, especially when you have partners," he said, "it's hard to put enough back into the company to grow."

When I asked him what changed, he said it was the control he had over where the money was being spent. He specifically noted the importance of investing in the people and into customer experience. He said, "Every touch point matters, especially with regards to sales. From when you hand them your business card, to what your brochure looks like, to what your PowerPoint looks like. To what their experience is with you, to what their experience is with your team, all the way through their experience with the company. That's one of the main reasons that we've seen client retention the way we have."

When Farhan was able to invest money into his employee engagement and customer retention, the economics worked themselves out. He cared about the people, and the money took care of itself.

MATT BERTULLI

In my interview with Matt Bertulli, who helped start Pela Case, he talked about how the product was invented in Saskatoon and now has a global reach. Saskatoon is no New York or San Francisco. He said, "We simply put the right people in the right seats and rebooted a brand with a clear mission to build a future without waste. We just had to find our customers, and once we did we had a business with great impact. We went from a six-figure business to a very fast-growing eight-figure business in a year and a half."

He continued, "We're living proof that you don't have to be a massive billion-dollar business to have purpose. The line I'm using now is that 'moon shoots aren't just for billionaires.' I believe that all profit is fuel for wherever we want to use it. People are willing to buy better things if they are shown better things."

Like Farhan, Matt was free to invest his money where he wanted to because his whole concept was based on purpose.

KELSEY RAMSDEN

Kelsey Ramsden has an amazing story. She was voted top female entrepreneur of the year by *Profit* magazine and was the CEO of a construction company. In an interview I did with her, she said, "I often try and introduce myself without all of the propaganda machine stuff, or how many children I've bred, or what schools I went to, or what degrees I have and all that stuff. I just say, 'My name is Kelsey Ramsden. I'm a creator and I deeply value truthful, intimate connection—to my work, to the people that work with and for me, and to the things that I create.'"

When I asked her how she measures profit, she explained that how she began was much different than what she believes now. Originally, she bought into the message that you have to be hardcore to gain respect. She said, "I would really grind people, and I would get a less than optimal result."

She continued, "I quickly realized that to be successful long term, I needed to be fair but firm. I wanted to understand each person I worked with, what drove them. I wanted to develop long-term relationships built on trust. In doing so, the work would require less of my personal time. When you have mutual respect, people will go the distance for you."

The results of being people-first have paid off for Kelsey. *Forbes* magazine called her the fifty-million-dollar woman.

CHAPTER 12

THE BRAND

In the previous chapter, we saw how profit means more than just quarter after quarter receipts. Part of the way you profit is by building a long-term brand.

How are you building your brand? If you're trying to buy it, you can't. Your brand is made up of experiences that your customers, employees, and community have when interacting with your company. Your brand isn't created by spending a million dollars on billboards or radio ad campaigns. Your brand is what customers think and feel when they see your logo based on their experiences with you.

Often, companies spend crazy amounts of time and money hiring branding companies to position them in the market. I see some value in that, of course, but it doesn't make sense to spend all that money and then neglect to build a People-First Culture. Ultimately, it's your culture that's going to create an authentic brand that can last a hundred years.

Think of trying to buy a brand like trying to buy popularity by having the nicest clothes and luxury cars when you act like a piece of shit. Will people connect with you authentically if you do that? No, because authentic connection comes from who you are.

The people who can say who you truly are—your customers, employees, and community—are the people who will tell you what they experience your brand to be. What do your customers think when they see your employees in uniform? What do your employees feel when they get their twenty-dollar gift on their first day?

Entrepreneurs and leaders tend to be achievers, and achievers tend to know how to manipulate situations to get what they want. However, this means they sometimes lack self-reflection. *Who am I? Who do people know me as?* Without this kind of self-reflection, an entrepreneur will have a difficult time understanding their purpose or their company's purpose.

In my conversation with Howard Behar, he noted that there are commonalities among successful brands. They all have a clear purpose. Starbucks, for example, has always been shaped around supporting people and working together—and people notice. They feel the purpose, and it becomes a shared value. According to an article in *Harvard Business Review*, titled, Three Myths about What Customers Want, 64 percent of people said shared values is the main reason they choose to patronize brands they love.

THE GROWTH OF OUR BRAND

In a very short period of time, we managed to build a brand on arguably the most competitive street for hospitality in all of Canada by living and breathing a People-First Culture. Before we opened, we built and deployed nineteen operational strategies to enrich the lives of our customers and employees.

Because of that, our brand is extraordinarily strong both online and offline. We don't have to pitch stories to the media; they come to us. There's a reason why the *LA Times* wants to rent out our building for the second consecutive year in a row as their headquarters for the Toronto International Film Festival. There's a reason why we've hosted events for Nike and American Express. If our brand wasn't strong, these companies wouldn't want to align with us, since that would be a negative reflection on their brands.

Our brand reputation takes down barriers and creates

opportunities to collaborate with other companies and work on joint ventures. We spend less than 1 percent of our budget on marketing. We don't need to spend more because we have organic growth. Our customers come back. They refer us to their friends and family. Remember, word of mouth is *the primary* way you grow a profitable company organically.

You know you have a truly amazing company when your employees regularly advertise on your behalf. Our employees are always asking us to come out with more merchandise. They want more hats and T-shirts with our logo on them, because they're proud to wear our brand.

Take Eric Lockwood, for example. He is a line cook and one of our most dedicated team members. I love this guy. He's a young cat and thrives in our space. Every time I see him, he has a smile on his face, gives a sincere "hello," and is uplifting in some way. I love getting to work with these kinds of team members who are free of entitlement and naturally advertise for the company.

"You know what I love about this company?" he said, as I sat across from him at our Employee Advisory Board Meeting. "This is the first company I've ever been proud to work for."

He told me a story of one time when he went to get coffee

wearing his Baro hat. The barista asked, "Do you work at Baro? I heard they are a great company." I smiled. The interaction made us both feel good.

IT TAKES PATIENCE

It takes patience to build this kind of brand. It takes patience to build word of mouth. But it doesn't have to take much patience. We went from zero to $15 million in one and a half years because of our People-First Culture. What takes patience is trusting that taking care of people will always pay a return, both in your personal and professional life.

Still, building a People-First Culture will take time, especially if you haven't been operating the way described in this book for a long time. If your company is forty years old and you now want to operate differently, you have to be ready to learn and put in the work. You have to rewire the entire organization, but changing is completely possible. Remember Lawyer Trane, the HVAC company I mentioned earlier? They had been operating for decades before they decided to truly focus on customers and employees. In a short time, they were able to build a People-First Culture.

The reason our company could catapult to success so quickly was because I knew the kind of company I wanted to build from day one. If you've been running a different kind of business with a different kind of culture for many years, I won't lie to you. It's going to be challenging rewiring the DNA of your company. I also believe you can experience some short-term successes if you start changing, even in little ways, now.

If you're aspiring to build a company, I encourage you to use this book as a model. Steal from me. Seriously. Do what I did from the very beginning. Make a People-First Culture the core of your company from day one, and within twelve months, you'll have an amazing brand.

Whatever situation you are in, know that there will be time required to invest in relationships. That's how life works. You can put the processes from Part Two in place and have the onboarding process ready to go for employees, but to become a sustainable business and a known brand, you have to build and maintain relationships. It all takes time.

THE POWER OF A BRAND

In a recent interview with Fast Company, TBWA's Neil Barrie provided insight into what brand is all about. I want to conclude this chapter with his beliefs about brand, which are directly aligned with my own.

He first discussed the process of identifying key brand attributes. He said,

> We asked ourselves, what do we mean by a truly iconic brand? The first characteristic is that they are instantly recognizable visually. You look at a Coca-Cola, at a Starbucks, and you recognize that brand wherever you see it. One of the first things my kid said was "Starbucks," pointing at a logo. The second ingredient is a universal value proposition. The third is that they genuinely play a role in culture. Apple, for instance, is not just taking from culture. They are actively driving culture. And then the fourth ingredient is, do they tap into higher-order values that transcend the product, and actually stand for something? The fifth is all about emotional connection, and that is really the root of it. That's where a brand like Disney has really benefited. It has leveraged the power of emotion. We make decisions emotionally more than rationally. Brands have a unique ability to tap into that decision-making.

From my perspective, value in a strong brand isn't one-dimensional. Your financial value is what your company produces every month on your balance sheet and profit and loss statement. Your employee value is the connection your team has with your brand. What sentiment do they have for the company before, during, and after their tenure with your company? The third value is related to community. What does the community think of your brand? I remember hearing someone say, "Restaurants should stop feeding the rich!" Did this person mean stop welcoming the 1 percent? No, he meant that restaurants (or any businesses) should give back by having a relationship with more than dollars and cents. The fourth value of a strong brand, developed by a People-First Culture, is customer value. Does your company give your customers such a strong value proposition in everything you do that you could sell them more than what you offer today?

CHAPTER 13

THE EMPLOYEE

Does a focus on the employee in a People-First Culture truly lead to profit? Let's begin by taking a look at a couple stats:

- A recent Gallup study found that highly engaged business teams result in 21 percent greater profitability.[7]
- Aberdeen found that companies with engaged employees see 233 percent greater customer loyalty and a 26 percent greater annual increase in revenue.[8]

What do these stats have in common? They each equate investment into employees with long-term financial gain.

---

7   http://www.gallup.com/reports/199961/state-american-workplace-report-2017.aspx

8   http://www.aberdeen.com/research/10985/10985-RR-customer-employee-engagement.aspx/content.aspx

EMPLOYEE PAY

The employee is a major part of the whole profit equation. When I joined 1-800-GOT-JUNK?, I was earning $10 an hour in the beginning as a call center agent. I was in my early twenties, and I couldn't do much with my salary. You can't take a pretty girl out to dinner on $10 an hour, but I had a long-term mentality. I left business school to work for 1-800-GOT-JUNK? because I knew it was an environment where I could learn how companies are grown from nothing to $100 million organizations and beyond.

When I joined the company, I quickly realized how much I was learning, and I knew that learning would equate to more money and success for me five or ten years down the road. I wired myself to think long term, so even though my initial salary was low, I avoided the thought of leaving. I knew I was going to be fine.

At Baro, I want my employees to feel like they're getting a better deal, because that's what I felt like at 1-800-GOT-JUNK?. At the time, I said, "I can't believe these guys are paying me to learn all this stuff so I can get my real-world MBA. I'm going to use this knowledge to build a $100 million company of my own one day." I knew I was getting a better deal. It was a case of meaning versus money.

PURPOSE OVER PAY

Is your company giving team members a greater sense of purpose and meaning as part of the team, culture, and community? Or, are you simply saying, "Why are you complaining? We pay you well. Come in and be quiet." You have to build a culture where people have meaningful relationships and a meaningful purpose with their responsibilities at work.

As mentioned earlier in the book, your company should be a springboard to success for your team members. It should lead them to success within your company. One day, maybe they'll want to grow from being a call center agent to vice president of marketing, or maybe they'll want to go off and do some other venture. Either way, you should care about their success.

Companies that have purpose at their core tend to have employees who have long relationships with them. They will also be inspired to do your recruiting for you. If you don't have to recruit as much and have low employee turnover, you won't spend as much time and money interviewing, educating, and onboarding. Since you're saving all that money, you're becoming more profitable, and you can do whatever you want with that extra profit. You can reinvest it right back into the company to get even better, quarter over quarter.

With purpose at the center, you will also profit from high employee morale. Do you want to come into an office that feels like an assembly line, or would you rather come to an office where people are genuinely happy? You can't underestimate the value of happiness within a workplace.

I recommend using a particular script or pitch to explain to potential hires why purpose is most important. When you do that, they end up leaving money on the table because they're more concerned with the meaning instead of the money they'll be making. This might rub some people the wrong way, but I'm fine with that. I take pride in having team members leave money on the table. Another company might offer them a salary that is $12,000 more, but they will say, "I'm going to work with Baro because they get it. They get me. I'm going to leave some money on the table just like Michel Falcon left money on the table when he was recruited away from 1-800-GOT-JUNK?."

From a profit perspective, our salaries aren't as high as our competitors, but we tell prospective employees our story when they come in. "Look," I'll say. "You're going to be enticed with more money from other companies along the way. I would like you to have a conversation with me before you decide to leave for that extra bump in salary. I want one last shot." I've been able to turn many people with that last shot, but I've also lost some people.

When I lost one of our cooks named John, who chose to leave for a dollar more in pay, I asked myself if we'd built a platform for John to choose purpose over pay. I know we have. While John certainly may have had his reasons for leaving, I tried to help him see long-term. The truth is that some people can see this way and some can't. Everyone is in a different place in life. My goal is to help my team members know their purpose and succeed. I have to let go of the reality that a little less money will sometimes be the deal changer. I have to keep my focus on the bigger picture.

Thankfully, many people naturally understand the message if you can show them the end result. I recently had a conversation with Jordan Lopez, the marketing expert I told you about earlier in the book. He said he knows he could make more money somewhere else. It would be as simple as going online and typing, "Marketing manager's salary, Toronto." He's leaving $14,000 on the table.

"Jordan," I said. "You have to eat dirt for a little while before you can eat caviar."

This is a message I believe millennials really need to hear. When they can hear the message and understand it, they are bound to be successful.

You might be thinking our salary model doesn't sound

very people-first, but it's important to note how we use the money left on the table. We invest it right back into the business. In fact, we often compensate team members in ways most companies never would. In the introduction, I mentioned how we once gave away $2,500 in gift certificates to Flight Centre, a travel agency, to four of our highest performers. That money came right out of my own pocket after taxes. I'm not Santa Claus, but I'm certainly not the Grinch either. It all balances out.

We also invest the money back into employee-facing initiatives that help us develop leaders through quarterly initiatives, books, and educational courses. Ultimately, our purpose over pay, long-term philosophy allows us to have a profitable business and invest into our growth. Our goal is for the assistant general manager to be equipped to become a general manager in the next business we open. We can only accomplish this growth with people who share our long-term philosophy of purpose.

EMPLOYEE SUCCESS

As I have shared in various ways throughout the book, you want to encourage your employees and bring them to success, whatever success means for them as individuals. This, too, creates profit. The success of a People-First Culture isn't defined by the entrepreneur or leader. It's defined by how successful the employees are.

One of the ways I contribute to employee success is through my Monday morning Breakfast N' Jam sessions. During these sessions, I'm able to give some advice to my team members. I've met with an employee named Kenroy, our rising star, twice this year. The first time, he was a newly hired floor manager.

During our interview process, Kenroy came to the group interview with one other person. The other person had a better resume than Kenroy, but he was arrogant. By his body language and short answers, we could easily see he didn't want to be there. We did not move him on to the skillset interview, which allowed Kenroy to shine. He was the shining star alongside a turd. The cream always rises to the top. From the start, Kenroy was engaged, and we knew he was the right one.

During this initial Breakfast N' Jam session with Kenroy, I learned that his goal was to become a corporate trainer in the hospitality industry. I needed to know that. I told him, "Kenroy, you should tell your manager. Your goal is now our responsibility. You will become a corporate trainer, I promise you, within the exact period of time you shared with me."

Later that same year, I met with him for breakfast again in the same location. I asked him, "What's going on?"

He said, "Remember the last time we met here?"

"Yes, of course," I replied.

"Well, I've changed my purpose in my career. I now want to be an assistant general manager."

He'd started in a floor manager position, so this was a sizeable promotion. Immediately after our breakfast, I found out from my general manager that Kenroy, by sheer coincidence, was going to be promoted to AGM. Kenroy had no idea. It was so fun to later share the announcement with him.

In the end, Kenroy's journey toward success was a win for us. Whether or not he would have chosen to stay, we benefited from having an amazing team member who was fully committed to our culture. We knew he would continue to recruit for us and help us with organic growth. The fact that he was promoted and stayed with us was just icing on the cake.

THE RESULT OF BETTING ON HUMANITY

Having this springboard mindset ends up being profitable for your business in the long run—every single time. Our general manager, Colin Denton, left us to go back to Vancouver and open his own restaurant. I didn't panic for one second. On the contrary, I felt joy for him. I also knew he would always have good things to say about us.

When people see your logo, brand, or employees in their uniforms, you want them to feel a sense of admiration. This admiration will benefit you in the long run.

At a conference once, someone asked me, "How do you prevent employees from trying to take your intellectual property and start their own thing?" My response was, "Who cares if they do?"

If you run a software company, you might be concerned about an employee stealing proprietary coding. If you run a restaurant, you might fear that people will steal recipes. I could easily fear that others might take my interview process, onboarding process, or education materials, but instead, I choose to share them openly. In fact, if somebody went into our Dropbox and downloaded all of our content, it wouldn't bother me. I would take it as a compliment. I would think, *Our proven systems that are giving the city of Toronto a great dining experience are going to be exposed to even larger audiences.*

The majority of people aren't going to do anything with your intellectual property anyway. And if they take something from you, what can you do? You can't protect yourself from every bad thing that could ever happen. You'd have to never cross the street again or go out in the rain. Some might think I'm naïve, but I'm simply choosing to bet on humanity. If I get screwed,

I get screwed. I'll bounce back, but I won't regret my decision.

Being people-first means you choose to trust your employees and believe the best of them. In my experience, this kind of trust helps build a culture that people admire. And admiration leads to profit.

CONCLUSION

When you first embrace a People-First Culture, you have to go through a paradigm shift. Once you internalize it, you experience a breakthrough. No longer is your purpose simply to be at the top making money. Your purpose is to bring others with you into success—to truly enjoy the process of building a business and benefit in return.

You may think you already have a People-First Culture, but I'd encourage you to dig deeper. When I hear people make that claim, I ask them to show me—the initiatives, the budgets, the breakfasts. Show me.

If you do legitimately have a People-First Culture, my encouragement is to not stop. The pursuit to put people first is never-ending. Customer and employee expectations will keep changing, and you have to be ready to evolve so you can stay ahead and exceed their expectations.

Sometimes, we need to reflect on businesses that haven't made it. These businesses didn't lose simply because of lack of technology. They lost because they lacked a purpose beyond profit. Don't become the next case study. Don't lose your shirt to your competitor. Look at companies that are getting it right, like Warby Parker and Netflix, companies winning with a clear focus on people. Know your purpose, implement the strategies I've shared with you, and win for years to come.

Today is the day to start. Are you going to be a good husband or wife? Do it today. Don't wait a year. Are you going to be a good friend? Do it today. Don't wait a year. In the same way, if you're going to create a People-First Culture, step up today.

Today is the day to keep going. If you've already built a Starbucks, then keep doing good work. The world will thank you.

You need to continually revise your systems and processes so that you stay relevant for decades to come. When you're putting people first, you're putting relationships first. When you're dealing with relationships, there is always more to learn.

I want to invite you to take a picture of the book and use hashtag #PFCulture and @michelfalcon to post on social media so we can continue this conversation online. I also encourage you to email me directly at michel@michelfalcon.com. Let's put the People-First Culture into practice together. Let me know what you're up to and how I can help. I look forward to talking to you!

This book is one step on my journey to further sharing the People-First Culture with the world. Where will I be two, five, or ten years from now? I have a few ideas, but I know one thing for certain: I will continue focusing on people. I hope you will too.

ABOUT THE AUTHOR

MICHEL FALCON is an entrepreneur, advisor, and international keynote speaker who leverages his People-First Culture™ philosophy to create customer experience, employee engagement, and company culture strategies to grow businesses.

He and his business partners operate a portfolio of restaurants and venues in downtown Toronto. Their venues have grown to earn tens of millions of dollars in revenue with more than one hundred employees in less than two years.

Michel has advised and spoken at conferences for companies like Alfa Romeo, Verizon Wireless, Electronic Arts, LUSH, and many other globally recognized brands. He was selected as the spokesperson for McDonald's Canada National Hiring Day campaign.

His writing and unique approach to culture has been featured in publications such as, *Forbes, Entrepreneur, Inc.* Magazine, *Time* Magazine, and Yahoo Finance.